Fresh 15-Minute Meals

BY THE SAME AUTHOR

Fifteen Minute Meals

Fast Italian Meals

Fresh 15-Minute Meals

Emalee Chapman

A PLUME BOOK

FOR DUNCAN,

WHO LIKES GOOD FOOD, AND IS ALWAYS IN A HURRY

PLUME
Published by the Penguin Group
Penguin Books USA Inc., 375 Hudson Street, New York, New York 10014, U.S.A.
Penguin Books Ltd, 27 Wrights Lane, London W8 5TZ, England
Penguin Books Australia Ltd, Ringwood, Victoria, Australia
Penguin Books Canada Ltd, 10 Alcorn Avenue, Toronto, Ontario, Canada M4V 3B2
Penguin Books (N.Z.) Ltd, 182–190 Wairau Road, Auckland 10, New Zealand

Penguin Books Ltd, Registered Offices: Harmondsworth, Middlesex, England

Published by Plume, an imprint of New American Library,
a division of Penguin Books USA Inc.
Previously published in a somewhat different form in a Dutton edition.

First Plume Printing, March, 1993
10 9 8 7 6 5 4 3 2 1

Ⓟ REGISTERED TRADEMARK—MARCA REGISTRADA
LIBRARY OF CONGRESS CATALOGING-IN-PUBLICATION DATA
Chapman, Emalee.
    Fresh 15-minute meals/Emalee Chapman.
        p.   cm.
    Reprint. Originally published: New York: Dutton, 1986.
    ISBN 0–452–26962–8
    1. Quick and easy cookery. I. Title. II. Title: Fresh fifteen-
minute meals.
    TX833.5.C43 1993
    641.5'55—dc20   92–30106
                                                   CIP

Printed in the United States of America

BOOKS ARE AVAILABLE AT QUANTITY DISCOUNTS WHEN USED TO PROMOTE PRODUCTS OR
SERVICES. FOR INFORMATION PLEASE WRITE TO PREMIUM MARKETING DIVISION,
PENGUIN BOOKS USA INC., 375 HUDSON STREET, NEW YORK, NEW YORK 10014.

Contents

Fresh 15-Minute Meals

Introduction

Yes, you really can cook a perfect meal in fifteen minutes. The secret lies in selecting fresh food and doing away with time-consuming preparations. The meals need only organized planning and practical shopping. This sensible approach to cooking is for busy people who want the best to eat, but have only minutes to spend in the kitchen. The emphasis is on seasonal produce from local markets—grilled, sautéed, or baked—and light sauces made with herbs and vegetables—quickly cooked so every ingredient retains its individual flavor.

Fresh 15-Minute Meals is for everyone who likes good food and enjoys entertaining; the uncomplicated recipes encourage the pleasure of sharing meals with friends and family. A simple menu can be prepared in a small kitchen with minimal equipment; even the inexperienced will have success. You will find yourself entertaining with confidence and speed. When it is possible to prepare an irresistible meal at home in minutes, why go to a crowded restaurant or stand in line for take-home food? All you have to do is unlock your front door, take off your coat, turn on the oven, assemble the meal, pour yourself a drink. While you unwind, your meal will be simmering.

SPECIFIC DIRECTIONS FOR SUCCESSFUL 15-MINUTE MEALS

TIPS AND METHODS FOR COOKING 15-MINUTE MEALS

You will find it easy to cook a meal quickly if you follow these specific and sensible directions.

1. Be frugal with your time and energy; eliminate time-consuming habits and rituals. When you step into your kitchen, preheat the oven or place a pot of water to boil before you start preparations. Use waiting time wisely: wash vegetables and fruits; make a sauce or dessert.

2. For successful fast meals it is essential to have sharp knives, heavy sauté pans and saucepans, a colander, sieve, and wooden spoons. All steps are accelerated by a food processor and/or blender. If you buy your equipment from a professional cookware supplier, it is certain to work.

3. Use pots and pans of proper size; if a pan is too big, there is too much exposed surface and the butter or sauce tends to burn or the liquid evaporates too quickly. Buy pots, pans, and baking dishes to suit your needs.

4. Wash all vegetables and lettuce carefully before using because of pesticides and dirt. Peel vegetables when necessary.

5. Slice vegetables and fruits into the bowl or cooking pan to catch all of the juices and to minimize cooking and cleanup time.

6. Whenever possible squeeze lemon, orange, and lime juice directly into the pan or bowl you are using in preparing a recipe.

7. Vegetables sliced fine or grated can be cooked in a few stirs around the sauté pan without any oils; diced and sliced pieces cook quickly, need just a bit of broth, and can be served with all their natural juices and vitamins.

8. Bone and slice fish, poultry, and meats; trim and remove skin and fat. Grill, broil, or sauté for fast cooking; the finished result will be tender and juicy.

9. When sautéing foods, smash or cut in half an unpeeled clove of garlic and place it in warm oil or butter; remove it after a few minutes, as soon as it has given off its perfume. Watch carefully, as garlic burns easily.

10. Use the clove of garlic unpeeled for gentle flavor; peeled garlic adds more strength.

11. Avoid using thickening agents: Sauces can be naturally thickened with chopped vegetables, and with fast cooking over high heat, the sauce will become reduced and concentrated.

12. Season to taste: Seasoning is vital, as much of the sensory excitement of food comes from seasoning. Use generous doses of fresh and dried herbs, freshly ground black pepper, paprika, and cayenne pepper. Beware of using too much salt, as many foods are naturally salty and add enough salt to the dish. In order not to overseason sauces, it is always better to taste and season them at the end of cooking.

13. Use unsalted butter in all recipes, as it does not burn as easily in cooking and does not add salt.

14. *Last, but not least:* All recipes, unless otherwise specified, are for 2; you can easily increase recipes, but please, allow more time for assembling, preparing, and cooking.

SHOPPING

Try to make your trips to the local markets interesting; look for seasonal vegetables, herbs, luscious fruits, and unusual breads. Experimenting with new foods, herbs, and spices can transform cooking from a chore into an adventure. Don't cook the same lamb chop and spinach over and over again. As the weather changes, your mood and appetite change—vary your meals, too. You have a multitude of choices. We live in a bountiful land.

Many independent farmers have begun growing vegetables and fruits that we used to find only in Europe. Small, specialized farms supply wholesalers, markets, and chefs with an extraordinary assortment of produce: doll-size carrots, miniature beets, turnips, and yellow tomatoes; tiny zucchini with blossoms still attached, miniature cauliflower and scallop squash, spaghetti-thin green beans, heads of red radicchio, and elephant garlic. An agricultural explosion has brought new produce to the smallest supermarkets and restaurants. How exciting to cook meals that make use of these vegetables and fruits, colors, tastes, and shapes.

Go to the market early, if you can, before the ripest and plumpest produce is gone. Twice a week buy vegetables and fruits that look bright and crisp to toss in soups and salads or pasta primavera. Shop at a large supermarket once a month to stock nonperishable items and to buy basic foods and ingredients that should be kept on your shelves for last-minute meals.

There are certain essentials that you should stock. Then when you have to resort to the can opener, these items will be within reach.

For the freezer:

spinach
green beans
peas
unsalted butter
frozen strawberries, raspberries

For the cupboard:

cayenne pepper
paprika
curry powder
dried herbs: basil, rosemary, thyme,
   oregano, tarragon
peppercorns: grind pepper fresh each
   time with a pepper mill
sea salt: adds texture and crunch to
   salads
vinegar, red or white; balsamic
olive oil (should be kept in a closed
   bottle in a cool, dark place; if oil is
   sold in a can, after opening
   transfer it to a capped bottle)
currant jelly
chicken broth, canned
canned salmon, crabmeat, lobster
canned white kidney beans for salads,
   bean stews
canned apricots
packaged dried pasta

For the refrigerator:

Parmesan cheese
Dijon mustard
eggs
heavy cream (ultrapasteurized cream
   does not boil well for sauces)

Appetizers

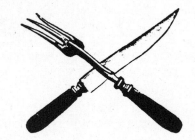

An appetizer should be something simple to tease the appetite; it should be well seasoned, not too rich, and not too much. The following pages provide many possibilities: hot hors d'oeuvres like Curried Bananas in curls of ham, Tiny Baked Tomatoes with Mustard Sauce, or cold Salmon Terrine made in advance. All stimulate the palate and whet the imagination for what is to come. Appetizers served at the table to start a meal are appealing, provide an attractive table decoration, and offer an invitation to sit down. Cheese-Roasted Peppers, Quick Crêpes wrapped around shredded vegetables, and Mushrooms with White Wine make quick and delicious appetizers. Of course, there is no reason why one can't enjoy a series of appetizers for a meal without bothering with a main course.

TINY BAKED TOMATOES

Experiment with tomatoes; they come in all shapes and colors: yellow, red, and green. Some have more juice and some more meat.

12 cherry tomatoes
2 tablespoons olive oil
1 tablespoon chopped fresh basil, or 1 teaspoon dried
12 small squares white Cheddar cheese

1. Preheat oven to 350°F.
2. Place tomatoes in a baking dish, and sprinkle oil and basil over them.
3. Bake for 4 to 5 minutes, shaking pan occasionally to turn tomatoes. (Tomatoes will be hot, not cooked.)
4. Serve on toothpicks with cheese and a bowl of Mustard Sauce (following recipe).

MUSTARD SAUCE

½ cup heavy cream
1 tablespoon Dijon mustard
Freshly ground black pepper

1. Place cream in a bowl and whisk until it stands in soft peaks.
2. Add mustard and stir to blend.
3. Season to taste with pepper.

CHEESE STRAWS

What could be more pleasant than to talk with friends, sip a drink, and be served a hot bite to eat? We sat grandly under potted palms in a London hotel and were served crisp, hot cheese straws.

Makes 10 long straws

2 tablespoons unsalted butter
½ cup flour
½ teaspoon dry mustard
⅛ teaspoon cayenne pepper
½ cup grated sharp Cheddar cheese
2 tablespoons sour cream

1. Preheat oven to 425°F.
2. Place butter in blender or food processor with flour, mustard, and cayenne pepper, and blend well.
3. Add cheese and sour cream and mix to form a ball of dough.
4. Place dough on an ungreased baking sheet and pat out to about a ⅛-inch-thick rectangle. Cut into 10 long strips.
5. Bake for 3 to 4 minutes, until straws are golden. Watch carefully, as they cook very quickly.

GOLDEN BISCUITS

Spicy seasonings make a delicate golden biscuit that adds piquancy to a drink or a light meal.

Makes 15 biscuits

3 tablespoons unsalted butter, at room temperature
½ cup flour
½ teaspoon curry powder
2 teaspoons Dijon mustard
⅛ teaspoon cayenne pepper
1 tablespoon milk

1. Preheat oven to 450°F.
2. In blender or food processor, combine butter with flour and quickly blend.
3. Add curry powder, mustard, cayenne pepper, and milk, and mix for a few seconds.
4. Place ball of dough on an ungreased baking sheet; press out dough with hands to ⅛ inch thickness. Cut with a 2-inch-diameter biscuit cutter into 15 biscuits.
5. Bake until pale gold, about 5 minutes.
6. Serve warm or cold.

FRIED CHEESE

This appetizer was served in a wine bar in Paris as we sampled the Sauternes.

1 small (8-ounce) ripe, not runny,
   Camembert or Brie cheese
Cayenne pepper
1 egg
2 tablespoons water
1 slice stale bread
2 cups peanut oil
3 sprigs parsley

1. Pare away much of the outer coating of the cheese, but do not remove all of the rind.
2. Cut cheese into wedge-shaped pieces; dust slightly with cayenne pepper.
3. Break egg into a bowl and mix with water.
4. Place bread in blender or food processor and make fine crumbs.
5. Dip cheese sections in egg mixture, then in bread crumbs.
6. Heat oil in a saucepan. Oil is hot enough when a small piece of bread turns golden quickly. Fry cheese in hot oil until golden.
7. Drain on paper towel.
8. Serve at once on a plate, garnished with sprigs of parsley.

CURRIED BANANAS

I first tasted this simple appetizer in Porto Ercole, a small fishing village near Rome.

1 banana
1 lemon
2 teaspoons curry powder
2 thin slices prosciutto
¼ cup chutney

1. Preheat oven to 375°F.
2. Cut banana lengthwise into 3 slices; cut slices in half. Place on a baking sheet.
3. Squeeze juice of lemon over bananas, and sprinkle on curry powder lightly.
4. Cut prosciutto crosswise into 3 strips to wrap around banana pieces, attaching each with a toothpick.
5. Place rolls on baking sheet in preheated oven and bake until prosciutto is crisp, about 4 minutes.
6. Serve at once with chutney in a bowl as a dip for the rolls.

SAVORY SHRIMP

This well-seasoned dish may be made a day in advance. It makes a spirited appetizer on rounds of toast, or a first course on endive leaves.

Makes 2 cups

1 tablespoon horseradish mustard
¼ cup red wine vinegar
2 tablespoons catsup
½ teaspoon paprika
⅛ teaspoon cayenne pepper
4 tablespoons olive oil
1 clove garlic, peeled
1 shallot, peeled
2 inner stalks celery
½ pound small shrimp, boiled and cleaned

1. In a bowl mix together mustard, vinegar, catsup, paprika, cayenne, and stir in olive oil.
2. Chop garlic, shallot, and celery and stir into bowl.
3. Add shrimp to mixture; cover bowl and place in refrigerator until ready to serve.

QUICK CREPES

When filled with a vegetable purée this makes a substantial first course or a light main dish. Crêpes are also good filled with raw shredded vegetables such as long wisps of scallions and carrots, with a little sour cream.

Makes 10 crêpes

½ cup flour, scant
1 egg
2 tablespoons unsalted butter, melted
½ cup plus 2 tablespoons water

1. Combine flour, egg, melted butter, and water in blender or food processor.
2. Use a 7-inch-diameter crêpe pan. Place over medium-high heat. Rub a drop of butter on bottom of pan with a paper towel, but do not butter pan heavily as butter will burn. When pan is hot, a drop of water will dance.
3. Pour 2 tablespoons batter into hot pan, tilting pan so that it spreads evenly into a thin pancake. Lower heat to medium.
4. Cook until bubbles form and crêpe is lightly browned, about 1 to 2 minutes; turn and cook about 1 minute.
5. Make crêpes as needed; batter keeps well if refrigerated.

5-MINUTE TOMATO SAUCE

This subtle tomato sauce with orange takes only 5 minutes to cook. Serve a spoonful inside rolled Quick Crêpes or prosciutto.

Makes 1 cup

1 tablespoon olive oil
3 medium-size ripe tomatoes
½ orange
1 teaspoon grated orange rind
4 thin slices prosciutto or ham, or 4
  Quick Crêpes (preceding recipe)
2 tablespoons chopped parsley

1. Warm oil in a sauté pan over medium heat; slice unpeeled tomatoes into pan.
2. Squeeze juice of ½ orange into pan, and add grated rind.
3. Cover pan and simmer about 2 minutes, until tomatoes are soft.
4. Stir tomatoes with a wooden spoon and mash with back of spoon to make a thick purée.
5. Cook over high heat to reduce liquid, about 3 minutes.
6. Place in blender or food processor and purée.
7. Spoon 1 to 2 teaspoons of purée into ham or crêpes, and roll.
8. Line up on a plate, cut rolls in half, and sprinkle with chopped parsley.

MUSHROOMS WITH WHITE WINE

This recipe can be served as a first course, or on small rounds of toast as an appetizer.

6 large mushrooms
1 shallot, peeled
4 tablespoons olive oil
2 tablespoons bread crumbs
½ cup white wine
Salt
Freshly ground black pepper
2 tablespoons pine nuts, chopped
2 tablespoons chopped parsley

1. Wipe mushrooms, or pass quickly under water, if needed. Remove stems from mushroom caps, and chop stems and shallot very fine.
2. Heat 2 tablespoons olive oil in a sauté pan over medium heat, add shallot and stems and cook 2 minutes, stirring continuously.
3. Stir bread crumbs into pan, add wine, and season with salt and pepper.
4. Remove sauté pan from heat. Fill each mushroom cap with cooked mixture. Place caps stuffed side up in sauté pan. Spoon remaining 2 tablespoons oil over caps and around them in pan. Sprinkle pine nuts and parsley over the caps.
5. Place pan over medium heat, cover, and cook 5 to 6 minutes until mushrooms are soft.

CHEESE-ROASTED PEPPERS

A colorful appetizer from Porto Ercole made of yellow or red peppers and served with crusty Italian bread, this is also a good accompaniment for meat or fish.

1 red or yellow bell pepper
2 tablespoons olive oil
2 tablespoons red wine vinegar
1 teaspoon dried thyme
½ cup grated Cheddar cheese

1. Preheat oven to 400°F.
2. Cut pepper in 4-inch strips, removing seeds and ribs, and place in a sauté pan.
3. Combine olive oil and vinegar, and pour over pepper strips.
4. Cover pan and cook over high heat 6 minutes.
5. Sprinkle grated cheese over peppers and place in preheated oven; bake about 5 minutes, until cheese melts. Serve at once.

SALMON TERRINE

A piquant appetizer, delicious with toast, slices of raw zucchini, or cucumber.

Makes 1 cup

One 3½-ounce can salmon, drained
2 tablespoons mayonnaise
4 sprigs parsley, stems removed
1 clove garlic, peeled
1 teaspoon Dijon mustard
1 tablespoon dry vermouth
1 lemon
Freshly ground black pepper

1. Combine salmon, mayonnaise, and parsley in blender or food processor.
2. Add garlic, mustard, and vermouth; squeeze in juice of ½ lemon, and blend well.
3. Season to taste with pepper.
4. Serve in a small bowl or a terrine garnished with the remaining ½ lemon cut in 2 pieces.

CHICKEN AND DUCK LIVER PATE

I first tasted this lovely pâté in the Chianti region of Tuscany, a sloping wooded landscape with cypresses, olive trees, and vineyards. Serve at room temperature on toast or crackers with a glass of red wine.

Makes ½ cup

¼ pound chicken livers
1 large duck liver
3 tablespoons brandy
1 bay leaf
Freshly ground black pepper
2 tablespoons unsalted butter
1 teaspoon dried sage
2 shallots, peeled

1. Place chicken livers in a bowl. Slice duck liver into strips and add to bowl.
2. Pour brandy over livers; add bay leaf and coarsely ground pepper to taste.
3. Melt butter in a sauté pan over medium heat.
4. Stir livers into pan, add sage and shallots, and sauté 3 minutes. Be careful not to overcook the livers.
5. Put livers and shallots in blender or food processor and purée.
6. Place purée in a small bowl or terrine.

Soups

Soup is versatile, nutritious, easy to digest, and simple to make. For centuries soup has been a complete and satisfying meal with bread and cheese.

Soups made with fresh vegetables that are quickly cooked and puréed are colorful and appealing: tomato red, spinach green, carrot orange.

One simple system of preparation in a blender or food processor yields a variety of soups that is limited only by the cook's imagination and supplies of fresh vegetables in the market.

There are endless possibilities: thick vegetable purées of broccoli, squash, lettuce (to name a few); thin broths; hearty hot soups; and refreshing cold soups.

Try consommé as a substitute for midmorning coffee or a hot broth for a quick pick-me-up. The recipes are fast and easy—the soup virtually is made in the blender or food processor. You will want to try them all.

GREEN ZUCCHINI SOUP

A light beginning to a meal or a midmorning snack. This soup is nutritious and refreshing almost anytime.

Makes about 4 cups

3 cups water
5 small zucchini, washed
2 celery stalks, washed
1 tablespoon chopped parsley
1 teaspoon grated lemon rind

1. Put water in a saucepan and bring to boil over medium heat.
2. Slice zucchini and celery into pan; lower heat to simmer and cook 4 to 5 minutes, until vegetables are tender.
3. Purée vegetables with broth in food processor.
4. Sprinkle with parsley and grated lemon rind before serving. Serve hot or at room temperature.

TUSCAN BEAN SOUP

A Tuscan country-style soup of tomatoes and basil, traditionally served with thick slices of coarse bread brushed with olive oil.

Makes about 4 cups

2 cups chicken broth
1 celery stalk, washed
1 cup canned lima or white beans
1 tablespoon olive oil
2 teaspoons dried basil
1 small onion, peeled
2 ripe red tomatoes, washed
Freshly ground black pepper
1/3 cup freshly grated Parmesan cheese

1. Put broth in a sauté pan and bring to a simmer over medium heat; slice celery into pan, and add beans.
2. Heat oil in a separate sauté pan, add basil, and slice onion into pan; sauté 2 to 3 minutes, until soft.
3. Slice tomatoes into pan; stir and simmer 2 minutes.
4. Stir tomato mixture into broth and simmer 5 to 6 minutes; season to taste with pepper.
5. Put soup in food processor and blend to a coarse purée; stir cheese into soup and serve hot.

GARLIC SOUP

This is a mild and subtle yet flavorful soup.

Makes 2 cups

2½ cups chicken broth
1 large potato, peeled
2 tablespoons unsalted butter
6 cloves garlic, peeled
Sea salt
Freshly ground black pepper
1 tablespoon fresh parsley or chives, chopped

1. Place broth in a saucepan over medium heat; slice potato into broth and boil gently.
2. Warm butter in a sauté pan and slice garlic into pan; cook gently for 2 to 3 minutes, until garlic is soft, being very careful not to burn garlic.
3. Stir garlic into broth and simmer 5 minutes.
4. Place soup in a blender or food processor and purée until smooth.
5. Season to taste with salt and pepper, and sprinkle with fresh herbs before serving.

YELLOW SQUASH SOUP

This bright-yellow, creamy soup can be served hot or at room temperature.

Makes 4 cups

3 cups chicken broth
4 green squash or yellow zucchini
2 scallions
½ cup heavy cream
1 teaspoon curry powder
Freshly ground black pepper

1. Pour broth into a saucepan and place over high heat.
2. Coarsely chop squash and scallions, and place in broth.
3. Boil rapidly over high heat for 5 minutes.
4. Place squash and broth in blender or food processor and purée. Add cream and curry and blend.
5. Season to taste with pepper.

ESCAROLE SOUP

An aromatic unstrained vegetable soup seasoned with garlic and thickened with pastina and cheese.

Makes 4 cups

3 cups beef broth
1 small head escarole
1 scallion
1 clove garlic
¼ cup pastina or any small pasta
½ cup freshly grated Parmesan
   cheese
1 tablespoon chopped parsley

1. Place broth in a saucepan over high heat.
2. Coarsely chop escarole and scallion, and add to broth. Peel and add whole clove of garlic.
3. Add pastina and simmer soup for 7 to 8 minutes.
4. Discard garlic, stir cheese into soup, and sprinkle with chopped parsley.

VENETIAN RICE SOUP

In Italy, peas represent the arrival of spring.

Makes about 3 cups

4 cups chicken broth
½ cup Arborio rice
2 tablespoons unsalted butter
1 scallion, chopped
½ teaspoon dried oregano
½ teaspoon dried basil
½ cup fresh or frozen peas
Freshly ground black pepper
½ cup grated Romano cheese

1. Place broth in a saucepan and simmer over medium heat; add rice.
2. Melt butter in a sauté pan; add scallion and sauté 2 to 3 minutes, until soft.
3. Stir herbs and peas into pan with scallion and cook for a few minutes, stirring.
4. Add mixture to broth in pan and simmer 5 minutes, or until rice and peas are tender.
5. Season to taste with pepper, and stir in 4 to 5 tablespoons of cheese; serve remaining cheese at table.

POTATO SOUP
WITH SWISS CHEESE

I ate this hearty soup in Switzerland while on a skiing holiday years ago, and it remains the best potato soup I have ever had. It makes a wonderful meal with a green salad, coarse bread, and good red wine.

Makes 4 cups

3 cups beef broth
3 medium-size white potatoes
1 shallot
4 sprigs parsley, stems removed
2 teaspoons Dijon mustard
⅛ teaspoon cayenne pepper
½ cup grated Swiss cheese

1. Place broth in a saucepan over high heat.
2. Coarsely chop unpeeled potatoes, and add to broth.
3. Peel shallot and slice into pan, and add parsley.
4. Boil rapidly over high heat for 8 to 9 minutes.
5. Place the vegetables and broth, mustard, and cayenne in a blender or food processor and purée.
6. Stir cheese into soup and serve at once.

CARROT SOUP

A bright-orange soup with a Mediterranean flavor that I had in Aix-en-Provence, where the food market takes up a whole square and the carrots are small and sweet.

Makes 3 cups

3 cups chicken broth
4 medium-size carrots, scraped
3 small white turnips, cleaned
Freshly ground black pepper
1 tablespoon fresh mint, chopped

1. Place broth in a saucepan over high heat.
2. Coarsely chop carrots and turnips and place in broth.
3. Simmer over medium heat 7 to 8 minutes, or until vegetables are tender; season with pepper.
4. Place vegetables and broth in blender or food processor and purée.
5. Serve at once in bowls with mint sprinkled over top.

SPINACH SOUP WITH POLENTA

Florentines make thick, nonliquid soups with vegetables and lots of cheese, and serve them with good bread.

Makes 3 cups

3 cups chicken broth
1 cup spinach, tightly packed
4 tablespoons coarse yellow polenta
1 cup freshly grated Pecorino cheese
Freshly ground black pepper

1. Place broth in a saucepan and simmer over medium heat.
2. Wash spinach, remove stems, and coarsely chop leaves; place in broth and simmer 2 to 3 minutes.
3. Add polenta a tablespoon at a time, stirring after each spoonful. Stir frequently while soup is cooking, about 8 minutes.
4. Stir ¼ cup cheese into soup, and season with pepper.
5. Serve soup hot in large bowls, and serve remaining cheese at table.

THICK VEGETABLE SOUP

A hearty country-style soup.

Makes about 4½ cups

3 cups chicken broth
1 bay leaf
½ small white cabbage
1 potato, peeled
1 carrot
1 small leek, cleaned
¼ teaspoon dried thyme, or 1 tablespoon fresh thyme, chopped
Freshly ground black pepper
⅓ cup freshly grated Pecorino or Romano cheese

1. Place broth in a saucepan, add bay leaf, and simmer over medium heat.
2. Put cabbage, potato, carrot, and leek in a food processor and coarsely chop into ½-inch pieces.
3. Stir vegetables into broth, add thyme and simmer 8 to 10 minutes until vegetables are tender.
4. Remove bay leaf and season with pepper.
5. Stir cheese into soup and serve hot with toasted bread.

FISH SOUP ANTIBES

I had this soup often in the old village of Antibes, near the Picasso Museum, in a restaurant that is popular with artists, writers, local politicians, and businessmen. The region's fish soups are liberally spiced with garlic and herbs. The fish shouldn't be overcooked, but left a little al dente. The firm-fleshed varieties need longer cooking than the delicate ones.

Makes 4 cups

2 tablespoons olive oil
1 teaspoon dried thyme
1 bay leaf
1 teaspoon saffron
1 tomato
1 small yellow onion, peeled
1 clove garlic, peeled
1 cup white wine
3 cups hot water
4 pieces fillet of sole or other white fish, such as sea bass or red snapper (½ pound), boned and skinned

1. Heat oil in a saucepan over medium heat, add thyme, bay leaf, and saffron.
2. Coarsely chop tomato, onion, and garlic and add to pan.
3. Cook over moderate heat for 2 minutes, stirring with a wooden spoon.
4. Add wine and hot water, 1 cup at a time. Remove bay leaf.
5. Place fish in pan and cook 7 to 8 minutes, until fish flakes.
6. Mash with spoon and stir to make a thick purée.
7. Serve with the Sauce for Fish Soup (following recipe) or Aïoli Sauce (page 23).

SAUCE FOR FISH SOUP

Olive oil, garlic, basil, thyme, saffron, fennel, bay leaf, and rosemary are employed with great skill along the Côte d'Azur. The cooking has a definite hint of the Italian. Italy lies just a few miles beyond Monte Carlo and Menton; the area was Italian much longer than it has been French.

Makes ½ cup

1 slice fresh white bread
1 large clove garlic
¼ teaspoon cayenne pepper
2–3 tablespoons olive oil
3–4 tablespoons broth from Fish
  Soup Antibes (preceding recipe)
Freshly ground black pepper

1. Place bread in blender or food processor.
2. Peel garlic and slice into blender, and add cayenne.
3. Add olive oil, bit by bit, or slowly in a thin stream, as you blend sauce.
4. Add broth to thin consistency of sauce.
5. Season to taste with pepper.

AIOLI SAUCE

Aïoli is the Provençal garlic mayonnaise that the people of Provence have loved since the days of the troubadours. Aïoli is served in the south of France, traditionally with fish soups and poached cod, usually accompanied by a selection of poached vegetables. It is used liberally with raw vegetables as an appetizer, with salads, and with poached white fish.

Makes ½ cup

1 egg yolk, at room temperature
¼–½ cup olive oil
2 cloves garlic
1 tablespoon red wine vinegar
Freshly ground black pepper

1. Break egg into blender or food processor and, as you blend, start adding oil, drop by drop, until egg and oil thicken to make mayonnaise.
2. Peel and slice garlic into blender or food processor, add vinegar, and blend well.
3. Pour into a bowl, and season to taste with pepper.

MUSHROOM AND CRAB SOUP

Makes about 2½ cups

2 cups chicken broth
12 large mushrooms, cleaned
1 shallot, cleaned
½ cup cream
2 tablespoons Marsala
6 crab legs
Freshly ground black pepper
¼ teaspoon paprika

1. Place broth in a saucepan and bring to a simmer over medium heat.
2. Slice mushrooms and shallot into broth and simmer 6 to 7 minutes.
3. Put cooked vegetables and broth in food processor and blend until smooth; return mixture to saucepan.
4. Place soup over high heat, stir in cream and Marsala, and boil for 1 to 2 minutes. Lower heat, add crab legs, and season to taste with pepper.
5. Dust with paprika before serving.

Egg Dishes

The egg is a cook's best friend. Its unique flavor and consistency bind, enrich, and give substance to a sauce and add a buoyant lift to cakes and soufflés.

Apart from its many splendid qualities in combination with other foods, the egg also is a meal in itself. In its simplest form, the egg is a worthy companion to the most sophisticated foods, and, as you can see in the following recipes, is cosmopolitan; I have gathered egg dishes from all over the world.

Eggs form the basis for many easily prepared, appetizing meals. The recipes are for simple dishes for oneself and friends.

Here are some suggestions about eggs:

- Simmer eggs; furious boiling toughens the whites of boiled eggs.
- Cook with room-temperature eggs.
- Egg whites can be beaten faster and stiffer in a small bowl barely wider than the beater than in a large bowl.
- If a raw egg floats in water, it is not fresh.
- Egg dishes are best when cooked in small quantity, and remember, omelets should be made for no more than 2 people and soufflés should serve no more than 8.
- Do not eat raw eggs.

FRENCH EGGS

This savory dish makes a meal with Carrot Soup (page 20).

2 eggs
2 tablespoons unsalted butter
2 teaspoons dried tarragon
½ pound small shrimp, cleaned
½ cup heavy cream
2 teaspoons Dijon mustard
Freshly ground black pepper

1. Put eggs in a saucepan and add enough water to cover them. Place over high heat, bring to boil, lower heat to simmer, and cook 5 minutes. Leave eggs in water.
2. Melt butter in a sauté pan over medium heat, stir in tarragon, and add shrimp.
3. Add cream and mustard, stirring to mix well. Simmer 2 minutes.
4. Remove shells from eggs. Cut eggs into thick slices, and stir into sauce.
5. Season to taste with pepper, and serve on toast.

SPANISH OMELET

Good served hot or cold with 5-Minute Tomato Sauce (page 11).

2 tablespoons olive oil
1 small yellow onion
4 small red potatoes
3 eggs
2 tablespoons water
Freshly ground black pepper
2 tablespoons chopped parsley

1. Warm oil in a sauté pan over medium heat. Peel and coarsely chop onion, and add to pan, stirring.
2. Place unpeeled potatoes in food processor with metal blade and finely chop, or shred on hand grater. Add to pan with onion.
3. Stir and turn vegetables as they brown. Cover pan and cook 3 minutes, or until vegetables are soft.
4. Break eggs into a bowl, add water, and whisk until combined.
5. Pour egg mixture over vegetables, cover pan, and cook 2 to 3 minutes, until eggs are set. Do not overcook. Omelet should be moist in center.
6. Season to taste with pepper; sprinkle parsley over omelet, and fold in half.

ASPARAGUS CUSTARD

12 medium-size, trimmed asparagus
  stalks, fresh or frozen
½ cup heavy cream
3 eggs
¼ cup grated Gruyère cheese
Freshly ground black pepper

1. Preheat oven to 375°F.
2. Place ½ cup water in a sauté pan
   over high heat. When water
   boils, add fresh or frozen
   asparagus and boil for 2 minutes.
3. Place asparagus in blender or
   food processor (reserving 4 tips
   for garnish) with cream and eggs
   and blend well.
4. Stir in cheese, and season to
   taste with pepper.
5. Pour into a lightly buttered
   baking dish (preferably a
   9-by-6-inch oval dish). Bake in
   oven for 7 to 8 minutes. (The
   custard should be soft.)
6. Garnish with 4 reserved
   asparagus tips, and serve at once.

NEAPOLITAN OMELET

Serve with Spicy Tomato Sauce (page
46).

¼ pound wide noodles (tagliatelle)
3 large eggs
½ cup grated Romano cheese
2 tablespoons butter
Red pepper flakes

1. Cook noodles in a large pot of
   rapidly boiling water 3 to 4
   minutes. Drain.
2. Beat eggs until well mixed, add
   cheese and stir in noodles.
3. Melt butter in a heavy skillet, add
   egg mixture and cook over
   medium heat 3 to 4 minutes; stir
   gently. Season with pepper.
4. When omelet is lightly browned
   on bottom, place on a warm
   plate and serve.

CORN PUDDING

This fragile custard makes a marvelous meal with a seafood or meat salad. Best of all, it cooks in a few minutes.

1 small red bell pepper
1 tablespoon unsalted butter
1 cup fresh-cooked corn kernels, or one 8-ounce can, drained
¼ teaspoon paprika
3 eggs
½ cup heavy cream
¼ cup freshly grated Parmesan cheese

1. Preheat oven to 400°F.
2. Coarsely chop red pepper, discarding seeds and ribs.
3. Melt butter in a sauté pan over medium heat. When butter foams, add red pepper, corn, and paprika. Mix and cook together for a few seconds.
4. Break eggs into a bowl, add cream, and whisk until well blended. Stir cheese into mixture.
5. Combine egg mixture and vegetables and put in a buttered baking dish (approximately 9-by-6-inch oval dish). Bake until just set, about 7 to 8 minutes. Do not overcook, as the pudding should be soft.
6. Serve warm or at room temperature.

MEDITERRANEAN EGGS

Brilliantly colored tomatoes and peppers are traditional staples of Mediterranean cooking. Cooked with fragrant olive oil and combined with herbs, cheese, and eggs, this makes a delightful supper dish.

2 tablespoons olive oil
1 medium-size red bell pepper
1 teaspoon dried basil
1 tomato
2 eggs
2 tablespoons cold water
¼ cup grated Monterey Jack cheese
Freshly ground black pepper

1. Warm oil in a sauté pan over medium heat. Thinly slice bell pepper into pan, discarding seeds and ribs.
2. Stir basil into pan with pepper, cover, and simmer 2 minutes.
3. Slice tomato into pan. Cover and cook for 2 minutes.
4. Break eggs into a bowl, add water, and whisk until well blended.
5. Pour eggs over vegetables in pan, add grated cheese, and season to taste with pepper.
6. Cover pan and cook for 2 minutes.

FRITTATA WITH ARTICHOKE HEARTS

Each time I land in Italy, the country delights me anew. I anticipate the marvelous restaurants and meals to be enjoyed. The Italians understand artichokes and know how to combine them with other flavors.

6 fresh or frozen artichoke hearts
2 tablespoons unsalted butter
½ teaspoon dried oregano
4 eggs
2 tablespoons chopped parsley
½ cup freshly grated Parmesan cheese

1. Preheat oven to 400°F.
2. Thinly slice artichoke hearts.
3. Melt butter in a sauté pan over medium heat. When butter foams, stir oregano and artichoke slices into pan and sauté for 2 minutes.
4. Break eggs into a bowl and whisk until well blended. Stir in cheese, reserving 2 tablespoons.
5. Pour egg mixture into sauté pan, and place in oven. Bake frittata in top level of oven 2 to 3 minutes, until barely set.
6. Sprinkle parsley and reserved cheese over frittata; cut into wedges, and serve at once.

ROMAN HAM AND EGGS

I had this in Rome for an al fresco
lunch, sitting on a terrace facing the
Piazza del Popolo, a glorious baroque
square. It makes a wonderful meal
with cooked green vegetables, bread,
and fruit.

6 slices prosciutto
4 eggs
½ cup milk
½ cup heavy cream
½ cup grated sharp Cheddar cheese
½ teaspoon dried rosemary, or 1
 teaspoon chopped fresh rosemary
⅛ teaspoon cayenne pepper

1. Preheat oven to 425°F.
2. Line a baking dish (approximately 9-by-6-inch oval dish) with
   slices of prosciutto, covering
   bottom and sides of dish.
3. Break eggs into a bowl and beat
   slightly. Add milk, cream, grated
   cheese, rosemary, and cayenne,
   and stir to mix well.
4. Pour egg mixture into dish over
   prosciutto. Place in oven and
   bake about 10 minutes. Do not
   overcook. The custard should be
   just firm, as the eggs will
   continue to cook after you
   remove the dish from the oven.
5. Serve at once with 5-Minute
   Tomato Sauce (page 11).

Potatoes, Rice, and Pasta

Rediscover the most popular root vegetable, the potato. The potato can be used as a basis for soup; as an accompaniment to meat, fish, or chicken; or as a salad.

- Potatoes retain nutrients better if cooked whole.
- Use as little water as possible when boiling potatoes.
- Choose uniform-size potatoes for even cooking. Avoid potatoes with wilted skins.
- The small red potato cooks quickly, does not need to be peeled, and adds flecks of color to purées and soups.

Rice for some is more important than bread. It can be a complete and satisfying meal simmered in broth with garden vegetables and garnished with cheese.

- Arborio rice is an imported Italian short-grain variety usually sold in small canvas bags. The long-grain variety doesn't give the same creamy texture to rice dishes.
- When making risotto, the chicken broth should be boiling hot when added to the rice.
- Stop cooking the rice just before it is completely tender, because rice continues to cook as it is carried to the table.

Pasta for nearly everyone is the most irresistible and addictive of foods. A dish of pasta can be beautiful, too, with the clear, bright colors of tomatoes, peppers, basil, parsley, herbs, and other vegetables.

How to cook pasta: There are two types of pasta, dried and homemade. The difference is chiefly in texture. The dried, packaged pasta imported from Italy, made of semolina flour with or without eggs, holds up better in cooking than fresh pasta and keeps indefinitely.

- A half pound of pasta serves 2 people as a main course, whether homemade or dried. Use at least 3 to 4 quarts of water for ½ pound pasta; it is absolutely essential to cook pasta in a deep pot with a large quantity of boiling salted water, so that it has space to expand and swim.
- Bring water to boiling, add salt, then instantly add pasta gently (without breaking) until all is submerged.

- Use a wooden fork to stir or separate strands as they cook. Dried pasta should be cooked for about 7 to 8 minutes. It comes in many thicknesses and shapes. Homemade pasta generally takes 2 to 3 minutes to cook, but angel's hair takes only a few seconds.
- Taste dried pasta after 3 minutes of cooking, and taste all pasta several times while cooking, until al dente, or slightly resistant.
- Drain pasta as soon as it is cooked.

POTATO PANCAKES

Try these with chopped chives, as suggested, or fresh herbs, or with a spoonful of chutney.

Makes 8 pancakes

1 large red potato, unpeeled
1 peeled shallot, or 1 slice onion
1 egg
¼ cup milk
¼ cup flour
¼ teaspoon baking powder
Salt
2 tablespoons olive oil
2 tablespoons chopped chives

1. Scrub the potato well and slice it and the shallot into blender or food processor. Add egg and milk and purée.
2. Add flour, baking powder, and salt. Blend until lumps disappear, about 5 seconds.
3. Warm oil in a sauté pan over medium heat. When hot, pour 2 tablespoons of batter into pan. Cook about 2 minutes on each side. Turn when golden brown.
4. Sprinkle chives over pancakes, and serve at once.

ITALIAN POTATOES WITH SAGE

On Elba there is an explosion of wildflowers in springtime. I like to be there on the Saturday night before Easter when this potato dish is served. The tender spring potatoes are the size of marbles.

3 tablespoons olive oil
1 teaspoon dried sage, or 2 teaspoons chopped fresh sage
10 small or 5 medium-size red potatoes
½ cup chicken broth
¼ cup freshly grated Parmesan cheese
Freshly ground black pepper

1. Warm olive oil in a sauté pan over medium heat. Stir in sage.
2. Coarsely chop unpeeled potatoes, and add to pan. Sauté 5 to 6 minutes, until golden.
3. Add broth and simmer over medium-high heat 4 to 5 minutes.
4. Stir cheese into potatoes, and season to taste with pepper. Cook 1 to 2 minutes, until cheese melts.
5. Serve at once.

FRENCH CREAMY POTATOES

In Paris near the Marais are the best vegetable pushcarts. One cart is filled with *mâche* (lamb's lettuce), endive, watercress, and every conceivable salad green. Another holds huge artichokes and a mountain of potatoes, large and small, piled in a pyramid.

2 tablespoons unsalted butter
1 tablespoon olive oil
5 medium-size red potatoes
½ cup heavy cream
½ cup grated Gruyère cheese
Paprika

1. Heat butter and oil in a sauté pan over medium heat.
2. Coarsely chop unpeeled potatoes, and add to pan. Sauté 3 to 4 minutes.
3. Pour cream over potatoes and simmer 4 minutes.
4. Fold cheese into potatoes and dust with paprika.
5. Cover pan and cook 2 minutes, until cheese melts.
6. Serve at once.

GREEN POTATOES WITH SPINACH

2 tablespoons unsalted butter
1 tablespoon olive oil
5 medium-size red potatoes
½ cup chicken broth
10 spinach leaves, washed
1 tablespoon red wine vinegar
Freshly ground black pepper

1. Heat butter and oil in a sauté pan over medium heat.
2. Coarsely chop unpeeled potatoes, and add to pan. Sauté 5 to 6 minutes, until golden.
3. Pour broth into pan.
4. Chop spinach leaves coarsely, discarding stems, and stir into pan. Simmer 3 to 4 minutes.
5. Add vinegar, cover, and simmer 2 to 3 minutes.
6. Season to taste with pepper, and serve at once.

YAMS WITH ORANGE

2 small yams or sweet potatoes
2 tablespoons unsalted butter
1 orange
¼ cup peanuts, chopped

1. Peel yams and slice into thin rounds.
2. Melt butter in a sauté pan over medium heat. Add yams in 1 layer and cook 2 minutes to brown.
3. Squeeze juice of orange over yams, cover pan, and simmer 5 to 6 minutes.
4. Remove cover and cook over high heat 2 minutes to reduce liquid and to glaze.
5. Sprinkle peanuts over yams and serve at once.

RISOTTO WITH FRESH HERBS

In Genoa, where much of the cooking is based on fresh herbs, this is a popular summer dish. Risotto should be creamy, not liquid.

2½ cups chicken broth
1 tablespoon olive oil
½ cup Arborio rice
1 scallion, chopped (2 tablespoons)
3 tablespoons mixed fresh herbs, such as thyme, oregano, marjoram, or tarragon
½ cup white wine
Freshly ground black pepper
2 tablespoons fresh basil, chopped
⅓ cup freshly grated Pecorino cheese
1 tablespoon parsley, chopped

1. Place broth in a saucepan and bring to a simmer over low heat.
2. Warm oil in a sauté pan over medium heat. Add rice and stir a few seconds, until each grain is lightly coated with oil.
3. Stir scallion into pan with rice, and cook 1 to 2 minutes, until soft.
4. Pour ½ cup hot broth into pan and stir; cook over medium-high heat about 1 minute, until broth evaporates.
5. Add ½ cup broth and stir; simmer 1 to 2 minutes, until broth has been absorbed.

6. Stir mixed herbs into pan with rice; add ½ cup broth.
7. When broth has been absorbed, add ½ cup white wine, and season to taste with pepper.
8. Use additional broth as necessary. Stir basil into pan with rice. When rice is al dente, remove from heat.
9. Stir cheese into risotto, and serve at once, sprinkled with parsley.

A creamy rice, to which the vegetables add flavor and color.

3 cups chicken broth
½ cup Arborio rice
2 small zucchini
2 small carrots
2 small yellow squash, if available, or 2 additional zucchini
Freshly ground black pepper
⅓ cup freshly grated Parmesan cheese

1. Place broth in a sauté pan, and bring to boil over high heat.
2. When broth boils, add rice. Lower heat and simmer.
3. Place zucchini, carrots, and squash in food processor with metal blade and chop fine, or grate with a hand grater.
4. Stir vegetables into rice and simmer 7 to 8 minutes, until rice is tender. Test rice by tasting. As soon as it is al dente, remove from heat.
5. Season to taste with pepper, stir in cheese, and serve at once.

RISOTTO WITH RADICCHIO

In Venice we went to the island of Burano, a charming and colorful fishing village far out in the lagoon. We had a classic risotto with radicchio in a small restaurant: thinly sliced radicchio with saffron-flavored cream sauce and freshly grated cheese.

3 cups chicken broth
2 tablespoons unsalted butter
½ cup Arborio rice
¼–½ teaspoon saffron
1 small head radicchio
¼ cup heavy cream
½ cup freshly grated Parmesan
  cheese
Freshly ground black pepper

1. Place broth in a saucepan over high heat and bring to boil, then reduce heat to simmer.
2. Melt butter in a sauté pan over medium heat. Add rice and stir a few seconds until each grain is lightly coated with butter.
3. Stir saffron into rice.
4. Pour ½ cup hot broth into pan and stir; cook over medium-high heat about 1 minute, until broth evaporates.
5. Add another ½ cup broth and stir.
6. Cut radicchio into thin slices and stir into rice. Add ½ cup broth and stir.
7. When broth has been absorbed add ½ cup more; after 1 minute test rice by tasting. Use additional broth as necessary. When al dente, stir cream into rice and add 3 tablespoons grated cheese. Carefully mix well.
8. Sprinkle remaining cheese over risotto, season to taste with pepper, and serve at once.

RISOTTO WITH SHRIMP

In Venice our fish was brought direct from the sea to the restaurant for our approval. We enjoyed a seafood risotto, salad, and amber-colored grapes.

One 8-ounce bottle clam juice
1 cup water
2 tablespoons unsalted butter
¼ teaspoon dried thyme
1 bay leaf
½ cup Arborio rice
1 small carrot
½ cup white wine
½ pound small shrimp, cleaned

1. Place clam juice in a saucepan with water and bring to boil over high heat, then reduce heat to simmer.
2. Melt butter in a sauté pan over medium heat and stir in thyme and bay leaf. Add rice and stir a few seconds, until each grain is lightly coated with butter.
3. Pour ½ cup hot clam broth into pan and stir; cook over medium-high heat about 1 minute, until broth evaporates.
4. Chop carrot coarsely and stir into pan. Add ½ cup broth and stir.
5. When broth has been absorbed, add wine to pan and stir in shrimp; cook about 1 minute, until wine evaporates.
6. Add ½ cup broth and stir. After 1 minute, start testing rice by tasting. When al dente, remove from heat and serve at once.

SUMMER SPAGHETTI

We wandered in the old town of Nice, where the streets are festooned with wash and lined with shops selling freshly made pasta and Parmesan and *dolce latte* (sweet milk) cheese. This recipe uses uncooked vegetables.

Sea salt
½ pound spaghetti
3 ripe tomatoes
8 fresh basil leaves
4 sprigs parsley, stems removed
4 tablespoons olive oil
3 cloves garlic, peeled
Freshly ground black pepper

1. Place 4 quarts water in a large saucepan over high heat and bring to boil. Add salt.
2. Add spaghetti to boiling water and cook until al dente.
3. While spaghetti is cooking, slice unpeeled tomatoes onto a large plate. Coarsely chop basil leaves and parsley, and sprinkle over tomatoes.
4. Bring oil to a simmer in a small saucepan over medium heat. Slice garlic and add to pan. Discard garlic when brown.
5. When pasta is ready, drain in a colander. Place pasta on a platter and arrange tomato mixture on top. Pour hot oil over tomatoes and pasta. Toss with wooden spoons.
6. Season to taste with salt and pepper. Serve hot or at room temperature.

CAPELLINI WITH SCALLOPS

In Naples, when exploring the streets and views above the city, I enjoyed this pasta dish in a small trattoria.

1 tablespoon olive oil
2 cloves garlic, chopped
1 shallot, chopped
½ teaspoon dried thyme
2 tablespoons parsley, chopped
4 mushrooms, thinly sliced
1 cup white wine
10–12 scallops
½ pound capellini
Freshly ground black pepper

1. Warm oil in a sauté pan over medium heat. Add chopped garlic and shallot and sauté for a few minutes, until soft.
2. Stir in thyme and parsley, add mushrooms, and cook 2 minutes, stirring to mix well.
3. Add wine ½ cup at a time; stir and boil sauce over high heat for 2 to 3 minutes, to reduce liquid.
4. If scallops are large, slice into 2 to 3 pieces; if small, leave whole; add to sauce and simmer over low heat 2 to 3 minutes, being careful not to overcook them.
5. Cook capellini in rapidly boiling water 3 to 4 minutes. Drain and place in a bowl.
6. Pour scallops and sauce over cooked pasta, season with black pepper, and serve immediately.

SPAGHETTINI WITH PROSCIUTTO

An absolutely glorious classic dish from Parma.

Sea salt
2 tablespoons unsalted butter
¼ pound thinly sliced prosciutto
½ pound spaghettini
½ cup heavy cream
Cayenne pepper
Freshly ground black pepper

1. Place 4 quarts water in a large saucepan over high heat and bring to boil. Add salt.
2. Melt butter in a sauté pan over medium heat.
3. Cut prosciutto into long thin strips and sauté in butter until crisp. Remove to a plate.
4. Add spaghettini to boiling water and cook until al dente.
5. While spaghettini cooks, pour cream into sauté pan and boil over high heat 2 minutes, or until cream thickens.
6. When pasta is ready, drain in colander. Place pasta in a warm bowl, pour in cream, and add prosciutto.
7. Season to taste with a few grains each of cayenne pepper and black pepper, toss, and serve at once.

CAPELLINI WITH FISH SAUCE

This has a lovely smooth sauce, with a wonderful combination of flavors.

1 cup white wine
1 shallot, peeled
4 sole fillets (about ¾ pound)
½ cup heavy cream
½ pound small shrimp, cleaned
¼ teaspoon paprika
3 tablespoons freshly grated Romano
  cheese
½ pound capellini
1 tablespoon parsley, chopped fine

1. Place wine in a sauté pan and bring to a simmer over medium heat. Chop shallot and stir into wine and cook 2 minutes.
2. Add sole to pan and simmer 2 minutes; remove fish and put aside.
3. Add cream to sauce in pan and boil over high heat 2 to 3 minutes until sauce thickens.
4. Stir shrimp into sauce and simmer 2 minutes; stir in paprika and cheese mixing until well blended. Add sole to sauce.
5. Cook capellini in rapidly boiling water 3 to 4 minutes. Drain and place in a bowl.
6. Stir fish sauce into capellini and toss carefully until mixed. Serve with a sprinkling of parsley over top.

FETTUCCINE WITH PEAS AND MUSHROOMS

In the hill towns of Umbria, one can still find feather-light golden strips of pasta (fettuccine or tagliatelle) prepared by hand each morning.

Sea salt
2 tablespoons unsalted butter
6 medium mushrooms
¼ cup fresh peas
½ cup heavy cream
½ pound fettuccine
½ cup freshly grated Parmesan
  cheese
Freshly grated black pepper

1. Place 4 quarts water in a large saucepan over high heat and bring to boil. Add salt.
2. Melt butter in a sauté pan over medium heat. Slice mushrooms into pan, add peas, and sauté 2 minutes.
3. Pour cream into pan and simmer gently.
4. Add fettuccine to boiling water and cook until al dente.
5. When pasta is ready, drain in a colander. Place pasta in a warm bowl, and pour sauce over it.
6. Add cheese, season to taste with pepper, toss with wooden spoons, and serve at once.

PENNE WITH ZUCCHINI

Sea salt
1 small red bell pepper
3 tablespoons olive oil
½ teaspoon dried thyme
4 small zucchini
1½ cups penne or other short tube
   pasta
¼ cup freshly grated Parmesan
   cheese
Freshly ground black pepper

1. Place 4 quarts water in a large
   saucepan over high heat and
   bring to boil. Add salt.
2. Slice bell pepper into thin strips,
   discarding seeds and ribs.
3. Warm oil in a sauté pan over
   medium heat, stir in thyme and
   bell pepper, and stir for 2
   minutes.
4. Place zucchini in a food
   processor or blender and chop
   fine, or shred by hand with a
   grater. Stir zucchini into pan, and
   sauté 2 minutes.
5. Add penne to boiling water and
   cook until al dente, 7 to 8
   minutes.
6. When pasta is ready, drain in
   colander. Place pasta in a warm
   bowl with 2 tablespoons of pasta
   water and stir in vegetables.
7. Add cheese, season to taste with
   pepper, toss with wooden
   spoons, and serve at once.

PASTA WITH RADICCHIO

Unlike southern Italians, the Milanese
do not dress mounds of spaghetti
with tomato sauce or olive oil and
garlic sauce. They prefer creamier,
richer pastas in smaller servings.

Sea salt
2 tablespoons unsalted butter
1 shallot, peeled
1 small head radicchio
½ cup heavy cream
Freshly ground black pepper
1½ cups short tube pasta, shells, or
   penne
½ cup freshly grated Parmesan
   cheese

1. Place 4 quarts water in a large
   saucepan over high heat and
   bring to boil. Add salt.
2. Melt butter in a sauté pan over
   medium heat. Chop shallot and
   add to pan. Sauté for 1 minute,
   or until soft. Cut radicchio into
   thin slices, reserving 4 or 5
   leaves for garnish, add slices to
   pan, and sauté for 1 minute.
3. Pour in cream and simmer 2
   minutes. Season to taste with
   pepper.

4. Add pasta to boiling water and cook until al dente.
5. When pasta is ready, drain in a colander. Place pasta in a warm bowl, pour on radicchio sauce, toss with freshly grated cheese, and garnish with reserved radicchio leaves.
6. Serve at once.

SPICY TOMATO SAUCE

This spicy sauce is from Capri. It is for any pasta, large or small.

Makes 1 cup

1 tablespoon olive oil
1 carrot chopped (2 tablespoons)
1 scallion chopped (2 tablespoons)
4 ripe red tomatoes, sliced
¾ cup white wine
3 tablespoons capers, chopped
12 black olives in oil (preferably Greek or Italian)
⅛ teaspoon cayenne pepper

1. Warm oil in a sauté pan over medium heat; add carrot and scallion and sauté for 2 to 3 minutes, until soft.
2. Add tomatoes to pan and cook for 1 to 2 minutes, stirring into vegetables; add ½ cup wine and simmer 4 to 5 minutes.
3. Stir capers into pan; add olives and simmer 2 minutes.
4. Season with cayenne pepper; add remaining wine and stir; cook 1 to 2 minutes. Serve hot over pasta.

CRABMEAT SAUCE

A good sauce for a fast meal; try it with ½ pound green fettuccine or spaghetti.

Makes about 1 cup

2 tablespoons olive oil
1 clove garlic
4 tomatoes
½ red or green bell pepper
Freshly ground black pepper
1 cup crabmeat, fresh or canned

1. Warm oil in a sauté pan over medium heat. Peel clove of garlic and add, stirring it in oil to brown slightly. Discard garlic.
2. Slice tomatoes into pan.
3. Chop bell pepper fine, discarding seeds and ribs, and stir into pan. Cover pan and simmer 6 minutes.
4. Mash tomatoes with a wooden spoon, and season to taste with pepper.
5. Stir in crabmeat and cook, uncovered, for 3 minutes.

RED-PEPPER SAUCE

In addition to being superb on pasta, this sauce can be stirred into vegetable soups and salads and is good on poached fish.

Makes about 1½ cups

1 tablespoon olive oil
1 clove garlic, peeled
1 medium-size red bell pepper, chopped
3 ripe red tomatoes, sliced
1 teaspoon crushed red pepper

1. Warm oil in a sauté pan over medium heat. Add garlic clove and stir until golden; remove and discard.
2. Stir bell pepper into pan and cook 2 minutes.
3. Stir tomatoes into pan and mix with pepper; cover pan and cook 1 to 2 minutes, until tomatoes are soft.
4. Stir crushed red pepper into sauce and mix well.
5. Purée in a food processor or blender until smooth.

Vegetables

Vegetables by themselves are my favorite foods, especially when cooked in simple, classic ways: I enjoy them alone, sautéed, braised, boiled, baked, or puréed uncomplicated by the presence of meat or heavy sauces.

Sometimes I make a meal of a combination of tender vegetables sautéed in oil, accented with an herb or two, and served quickly from the pan so none of the juices are lost. A dish of sliced fennel, tomatoes, and green beans served warm, with good bread, makes a feast.

Your vegetable dishes will depend on the season and what you find at the market. Look carefully for those vegetables that are brightly colored and firm to the touch. Cooked and seasoned with care, they will retain their garden freshness.

Remember:

- Wash vegetables quickly under cold running water; don't soak them.
- Vegetables are best cooked briefly in a minimum of liquid.
- Save and use vegetable broth for soups and sauces.

QUICK VEGETABLE IDEAS

- Grate or shred carrots and white turnips and sauté briefly in butter.
- Mash a grated carrot and finely chopped watercress with butter; spread between slices of whole wheat bread to make a vegetable sandwich.
- When you see a bunch of the early, very thinnest asparagus, serve either quickly blanched or raw with a sauce. To make an easy piquant sauce, blend until smooth a little sour cream and 1 teaspoon each of mustard and dried basil.
- When you find green beans at their tiniest, snap off the ends and sauté them in a little olive oil with garlic and fresh ginger; season with soy sauce.
- Lightly steam scallions and serve warm with mayonnaise thinned with lemon or orange juice.
- Yogurt flavored with garlic or chopped fresh herbs makes a creamy dressing for cooked green beans, asparagus, peas, or cauliflower.

THE ONION FAMILY: ONIONS, SHALLOTS, LEEKS, AND GARLIC

Along the European Mediterranean shore—Provence, the Côte d'Azur, southwest France, and northern Italy—in lusty, simple cooking, garlic is a necessity, adored and glorified. For the classic, more subtle French and northern Italian dishes, the shallot is preferred for its delicate flavor. In Turkey, Greece, and the Middle East, onions are one of the basic ingredients for most dishes.

Onions vary in size, color, shape, and flavor: large, sweet red onions; yellow onions; tiny white, and torpedo-shaped onions. The larger they grow, the milder they become.

Scallions are most commonly used in salads in the United States. The Chinese cut them in long, thin strips and scatter them over steamed fish and broth, making delicate patterns.

Garlic should be treated carefully. A gentle hint of garlic is achieved by using whole cloves, unpeeled. Cutting unpeeled cloves in half, exposing only one surface per piece, adds more strength. Peeling cloves makes the taste even stronger.

The frying and sautéing of garlic must be carefully done; the smaller the bits of garlic, the more critical the timing. Garlic should never be hastily cooked and should not be burned; it should never take on any hint of blackness. The longer garlic is cooked, the milder it becomes, as in soups and stews.

Whole peeled cloves of garlic roasted around a chicken or a leg of lamb can be mashed into the gravy for a savory sauce. Unpeeled cloves of garlic cooked slowly in the oven make a sweet and rich purée that can be spread onto a piece of coarse bread for a surprisingly mild accompaniment to soups or salads.

BELL PEPPERS VINAIGRETTE

Bell peppers are brilliant green at maturity and turn red as they ripen. The yellow variety are equally flavorful. Eaten raw, peppers add a crisp touch to salads and crudités. When cooked, their flavors deepen and intensify. Peppers are good with fish, poultry, and meat.

1 red bell pepper
1 yellow bell pepper
½ cup olive oil
3 tablespoons vinegar
1 teaspoon Dijon mustard
4 anchovies
Freshly ground black pepper
1 tablespoon capers
1 tablespoon chopped parsley

1. Cut each bell pepper into 1-inch-wide strips, discarding seeds and ribs, and place in a sauté pan.
2. Combine oil, vinegar, mustard, anchovies, and black pepper to taste, and pour over peppers.
3. Place sauté pan over medium heat and simmer 5 to 6 minutes, until peppers are soft.
4. Add capers and serve at once, sprinkled with parsley.

GLAZED WINTER VEGETABLES

The winter vegetables in Parisian markets are arranged in orderly rows: fat stalks of celery rest next to creamy white cauliflower; rosy turnips and bright carrots are placed beside the ruffled green leaves of Swiss chard.

1 small celery root, peeled
2 small turnips, scraped
2 small carrots, scraped
2 cups chicken broth
2 tablespoons butter
2 teaspoons sugar
Freshly ground black pepper
1 tablespoon chopped parsley

1. Cut celery root, turnips, and carrots into 1-inch-thick slices.
2. Pour broth into a saucepan and place over medium heat. When simmering, add vegetables and butter. Cover and simmer gently 6 minutes. Add sugar.
3. Remove lid and boil vegetables 2 minutes over high heat, stirring to prevent sticking.
4. When vegetables are tender and sauce is reduced to a thick syrupy glaze, season to taste with pepper and sprinkle with parsley.
5. Serve at once.

GLAZED CARROTS

Carrots are plentiful and adaptable. They can be used as crudités, grated in salads, puréed in soups, sliced as a vegetable, or baked into tea bread.

4 medium-size carrots, scraped
½ cup water
1 orange
¼ cup honey
2 tablespoons unsalted butter
1 teaspoon grated orange rind
¼ teaspoon powdered ginger

1. Cut carrots into 1-inch-long pieces, and place in a sauté pan.
2. Pour water into sauté pan, squeeze in juice of orange, and add honey and butter. Add orange rind and ginger.
3. Simmer over medium heat 5 to 6 minutes, until carrots are tender.
4. Cook over high heat, shaking pan, until liquid is reduced, about 2 minutes, and carrots are glazed.
5. Serve at once.

CELERY ROOT WITH PARSLEY

1 large celery root, peeled
1 lemon
2 tablespoons unsalted butter
1 cup chicken broth
2 tablespoons chopped parsley
Freshly ground black pepper

1. Cut celery root in thin rounds into a sauté pan. Squeeze juice of lemon over slices, and add butter and broth.
2. Place pan over high heat, bring to boil, cover pan, and simmer 5 minutes.
3. Remove cover and cook until golden and liquid evaporates, 2 to 3 minutes.
4. Stir in parsley, season to taste with pepper, and serve at once.

BROCCOLI WITH CHEESE

The Italians often season green
vegetables with cheese.

3–4 stalks broccoli
2 tablespoons olive oil
1 tablespoon wine vinegar
½ cup freshly grated Parmesan
  cheese
Freshly ground black pepper

1. Cut off and discard about 2
   inches from the bottom of each
   stalk of broccoli. Slice remaining
   pieces of broccoli lengthwise,
   through the florets, into 3 pieces.
2. Place 2 cups water in a sauté pan
   over medium heat and bring to a
   boil.
3. Add broccoli, reduce heat, and
   simmer about 4 minutes, until
   tender.
4. Place broccoli on a plate.
   Sprinkle oil, vinegar, and cheese
   over hot broccoli, season to taste
   with pepper, and serve at once.

ASPARAGUS WITH CHEESE

10 stalks asparagus
3 tablespoons safflower oil
¼ cup freshly grated Parmesan or
  Romano cheese
Freshly ground black pepper

1. Remove about 2 inches of tough
   lower part of asparagus stalks.
   Remove scales and cut diagonally
   into 1-inch-long pieces.
2. Warm oil in a sauté pan over
   medium heat, add asparagus, and
   sauté for a few seconds.
3. Add ¼ cup water and cook 3 to
   4 minutes, until asparagus are
   barely tender. Add more water if
   water evaporates before
   asparagus are cooked.
4. Stir in grated cheese, season to
   taste with pepper, and serve at
   once from pan.

SPINACH WITH CHEESE

1 large bunch fresh spinach
1 tablespoon unsalted butter
8 small white mushrooms
½ cup freshly grated Pecorino cheese
Freshly ground black pepper

1. Wash spinach and remove any tough stems; place wet spinach in a sauté pan.
2. Place pan over high heat, and cook, stirring, for 1 minute.
3. Transfer spinach to a blender or food processor and purée.
4. Melt butter in sauté pan over medium heat, slice mushrooms into pan, and sauté for 1 minute.
5. Add spinach, and cook for 1 minute with mushrooms.
6. Stir in grated cheese, season to taste with pepper, and serve at once.

SQUASH SAUTE

Summer squash, green zucchini, and yellow crookneck squash should be slender, young, and brightly colored. When older, they are tough and have seeds.

2 tablespoons olive oil
1 medium-size ripe tomato
2 small zucchini
2 summer squash
1 yellow crookneck squash
¼ teaspoon dried basil, or 1 tablespoon chopped fresh basil
¼ teaspoon dried thyme, or 1 sprig fresh thyme
¼ teaspoon dried oregano, or 1 sprig fresh oregano
Freshly ground black pepper
1 tablespoon chopped parsley

1. Warm oil in a sauté pan over medium heat.
2. Cut unpeeled tomato into ½-inch chunks, and add to pan. Cover and cook 2 minutes.
3. Slice unpeeled squash into ¼-inch pieces and add to pan. Sprinkle with basil, thyme, and oregano.
4. Cook vegetables until squash is tender, about 4 minutes.
5. Season with pepper and sprinkle with parsley. Serve at once.

SPINACH WITH PROSCIUTTO

The colorful section of Rome, Trastevere, where I found this dish, is ancient Rome. The walls, streets, and buildings were built centuries ago.

2 cups raw spinach leaves, to yield 1 cup cooked spinach
1 tablespoon olive oil
4 slices prosciutto, or thin slices of ham
2 tablespoons golden raisins
½ teaspoon grated orange rind
Freshly ground black pepper

1. Cut stems from spinach and coarsely chop leaves; wash under running water.
2. Place wet spinach in a sauté pan and cook over high heat 1 to 2 minutes, stirring. Drain in colander to remove excess water.
3. Heat oil in a sauté pan over medium heat; cut prosciutto into thin strips and sauté for 1 to 2 minutes.
4. Stir spinach into pan; add raisins and grated orange rind and mix well.
5. Season to taste with pepper and serve hot.

BRAISED LETTUCE

The clever French often braise leftover lettuce leaves or a whole head of lettuce, celery, fennel, or leeks.

15 lettuce leaves (can be a variety of lettuces)
1 cup chicken broth
1 tablespoon unsalted butter
Sea salt
Freshly ground black pepper
1 tablespoon chopped chives

1. Chop lettuce coarsely.
2. Pour chicken broth into a sauté pan, and add butter and lettuce. Place over medium heat, bring to a boil, and cook rapidly 3 to 4 minutes.
3. Season to taste with salt and pepper, sprinkle with chives, and serve at once.

BRAISED CELERY

Celery has such a mild fresh taste, it is best raw or cooked gently and dressed lightly.

6 tender inner stalks celery
1 cup chicken broth
1 tablespoon unsalted butter
¼ cup heavy cream
1 teaspoon Dijon mustard
Freshly ground black pepper

1. Cut celery diagonally into ½-inch pieces.
2. Pour broth into a sauté pan and place over medium heat. Add celery and butter. Bring liquid to boil and cook over high heat, about 5 minutes.
3. Combine cream and mustard, and stir into pan. Cook 2 to 3 minutes, until cream is reduced.
4. Season to taste with pepper, and serve at once.

BRAISED BELGIAN ENDIVE

Belgian endive is an elegant green vegetable prized the world over. In Belgium the most popular way to eat endive is braised and served hot.

2 tablespoons unsalted butter
4 medium-size Belgian endives
¼ cup water
1 lemon

1. Melt butter in a sauté pan over medium heat.
2. Cut endives in half lengthwise, and place in pan. Add water, and squeeze juice of lemon over endives.
3. Cover tightly and simmer 6 to 8 minutes, until endives are tender.
4. Serve at once.

FENNEL NICOISE

In the old quarter of Nice the market has an appealing scent of its own: there are baskets of bright-purple garlic and large red and white onions and pyramids of fennel with feathery green leaves.

1 red onion, peeled
1 fennel bulb, trimmed
2 tablespoons olive oil
1 clove garlic
½ teaspoon dried thyme
2 small ripe tomatoes
½ cup dry white wine
Freshly ground black pepper

1. Chop onion and fennel coarsely, including leafy tops of fennel.
2. Warm oil in a sauté pan over medium heat. Cut unpeeled garlic clove in half, and place, cut side down, in warm oil. Stir in thyme, add fennel and onion.
3. Coarsely slice unpeeled tomatoes into pan. Stir with fennel for 30 seconds. Discard garlic.
4. Add white wine and simmer 8 to 10 minutes.
5. Season to taste with pepper, and serve at once or at room temperature.

ARTICHOKES PROVENCALE

Fresh produce from the farms of Provence includes incredibly thin green beans, wonderful herbs, tender spinach, young peas, tiny shallots, potatoes, watercress, and artichokes.

2 firm, fresh artichokes
1 cup dry white wine
1 clove garlic
¼ cup olive oil
1 bay leaf
½ teaspoon dried thyme

1. Cut artichokes into quarters, discard the chokes, and cut the top third from each piece.
2. Place wine in a sauté pan over medium heat, and add unpeeled garlic clove, oil, bay leaf, and thyme.
3. When the liquid boils, add artichoke quarters, cover pan, and simmer 8 to 10 minutes. (If liquid is too reduced, add a little more white wine.) Discard garlic and bay leaf.
4. Serve artichokes with cooking liquid as a sauce.

SCALLIONS OR LEEKS BY THE BUNCH

Leeks can be sliced and eaten raw in salads, poached and served warm with olive oil and lemon juice, puréed, or braised.

1 bunch scallions, or 4 small leeks
2 cups water or chicken broth
3 tablespoons olive oil
1 lemon
2 teaspoons red wine vinegar
Sea salt
Freshly ground black pepper

1. Wash scallions or leeks well to remove all traces of dirt. Slice each in half lengthwise and reserve 2 green stems.
2. Make 2 bundles and tie with reserved green stems.
3. Place 2 cups of water or broth in a sauté pan over medium heat. When water or broth boils, add scallions or leeks. Cook 5 to 6 minutes, until tender.
4. Place on a plate to cool.
5. Pour oil into a bowl, squeeze in juice of lemon, add vinegar, and season to taste with salt and pepper.
6. Pour vinaigrette sauce over scallions or leeks, and serve.

CORN FRITTERS

1 cup cooked fresh or canned corn kernels
1 egg
4 tablespoons heavy cream
4 tablespoons flour
1 teaspoon baking powder
2 tablespoons chopped green chiles (canned)
2 tablespoons unsalted butter
Sea salt
Freshly ground black pepper

1. Place corn in a bowl. Beat egg and stir in with cream, flour, baking powder, and chiles. Mix well to make a thick batter.
2. Place 1 tablespoon butter in sauté pan over medium heat, and tilt pan so butter covers bottom.
3. Drop 2 to 3 tablespoonfuls of the corn mixture into pan, spreading them slightly with a spatula to flatten them.
4. Cook 2 to 3 minutes on each side, until golden brown. When butter browns, wipe out pan with paper towel, add remaining tablespoon butter, and cook more fritters. Drain on paper towel.
5. Season to taste with salt and pepper, and serve at once.

PUMPKIN FRITTERS

The northern Italians often use pumpkin in cooking, and often make pumpkin fritters. They are good with veal, fish, and chicken dishes.

1 egg
¼ cup milk
½ cup flour
1 teaspoon baking powder
½ cup canned pumpkin purée
2 tablespoons safflower oil

1. Break egg into a bowl and beat until light. Add milk, flour, and baking powder.
2. Fold in pumpkin purée.
3. Warm oil in a sauté pan over medium heat. Drop 2 to 3 tablespoons of pumpkin mixture into the hot oil.
4. Cook 2 to 3 minutes on each side, until golden brown.
5. Serve at once.

TURNIPS WITH CHIVES

6 medium white turnips
3 tablespoons sour cream or plain yogurt
1 tablespoon lemon juice
2 tablespoons chopped chives
½ teaspoon paprika

1. Place 4 cups water in a saucepan and bring to boil over high heat.
2. Peel and slice turnips and place in boiling water. Reduce heat and simmer 5 to 6 minutes, until turnips are tender.
3. Place sour cream in a bowl; add lemon juice, chives, and paprika and blend thoroughly.
4. When turnips are tender, drain and stir into bowl.

GREEN PEA PUREE

Vegetable purées, easy to cook and wonderfully colorful, are good accompaniments to chicken, veal, pork, and chops. Almost any vegetables can be puréed—spinach, turnips, carrots, green beans—then enriched with butter or cream and freshly grated Parmesan cheese.

1 package frozen green peas
1 sprig fresh mint
3 lettuce leaves
1 tablespoon heavy cream
Freshly ground black pepper
¼ cup grated Parmesan cheese

1. Place 2 cups water in a sauté pan over medium heat.
2. When water boils, add frozen peas, mint, and lettuce. Cook 4 to 5 minutes, until peas are tender.
3. Drain peas in a colander, and place in blender or food processor to purée.
4. Return purée to sauté pan, stirring over medium heat so any liquid will evaporate. Add cream, and season to taste with pepper.
5. Add cheese, and serve at once.

CABBAGE PUREE

Good with sausage, ham, and pork.

½ small white cabbage
4 small red potatoes
1 teaspoon dried thyme
1 bay leaf
1 tablespoon unsalted butter
Freshly ground black pepper

1. Coarsely chop cabbage and unpeeled potatoes.
2. Place 2 cups water in a saucepan over medium heat. Add vegetables, thyme, and bay leaf.
3. Bring to a boil, cover pan, and simmer over medium-high heat 7 to 8 minutes.
4. Drain vegetables in a colander, discard bay leaf, and place in blender or food processor to purée.
5. Return purée to saucepan, stirring over high heat. Stir in butter, and season to taste with pepper.
6. Serve at once from pan.

good

ONION-POTATO PUREE

This enhances any veal or lamb dish.

2 yellow onions, peeled
4 medium-size potatoes, peeled
2 tablespoons unsalted butter
1 tablespoon chopped fresh sage, or
  1 teaspoon dried sage
1 cup chicken broth
¼ cup sour cream
Salt
Freshly ground black pepper

1. Coarsely chop onions and
   potatoes.
2. Melt butter in a sauté pan over
   medium heat, and stir in sage.
3. Add vegetables and broth, cover
   pan, and simmer 6 minutes.
   Remove cover and boil rapidly 3
   to 4 minutes until vegetables are
   tender and liquid has reduced.
4. Purée vegetables in food
   processor. Add sour cream, and
   season to taste with salt and
   pepper.
5. Serve at once.

Fish

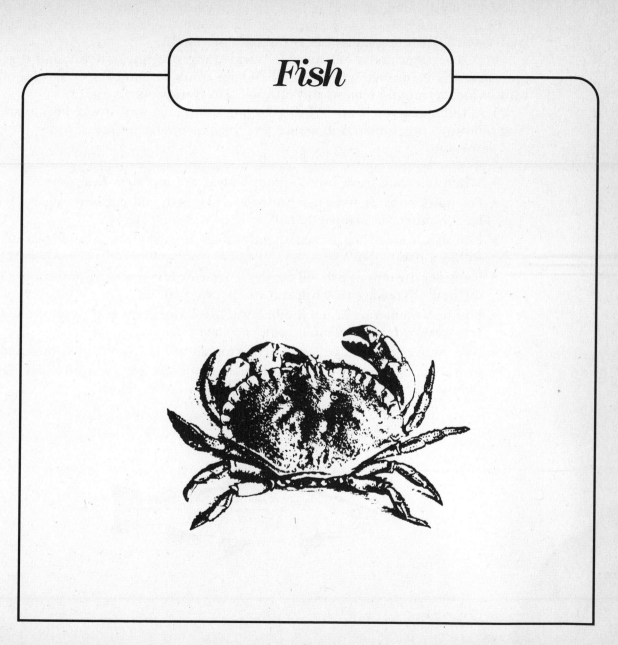

There are almost endless ways to cook, eat, and enjoy fish: grilled, broiled, sautéed briefly, poached, baked, or steamed. But the secret of moist and succulent fish is fresh fish of the best quality that is carefully prepared.

Fish is versatile and is enhanced by a wide variety of spices, herbs, and vegetables: saffron, dill, tarragon, thyme, basil, fennel, tomatoes, and celery. Basting with white wine, vermouth, lemon, and olive oil also brings out flavor.

You will find a vast array of fish glittering on ice in a well-stocked fish market. The following suggestions will assure you fresh, properly prepared fish. Remember:

- When selecting fresh fish, look for a clear eye and firm flesh.
- For quick cooking have fish boned and skinned, and cut large slices of sea bass, halibut, or snapper in half or in 3-by-3-inch strips.
- Fish should smell like the sea, slightly saline (not fishy), and should be cooked within a day.
- Consider the type of fish, oily or dry, coarse or fine-textured, and choose the method of cooking that will suit its special qualities.
- Poach in simmering liquid (boiling will break the flesh) and flavor the liquid with seaweed, herbs, lemon, wine, or clam juice.
- Bake in oven at 450°F wrapped in parchment or foil to cook in its own juices.
- Fish is done when it is opaque and flakes easily when tested with a fork. Only then season with salt, if desired.

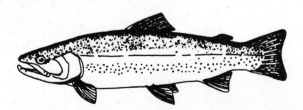

OYSTERS WITH PARMESAN CHEESE

In the old part of Nice there is a fish market with a blue awning. It has everything, including oysters and other kinds of shellfish. I went there often to buy oysters to take home and use in this savory dish.

1 tablespoon unsalted butter
16 oysters
1 tablespoon chopped parsley
1 teaspoon paprika
½ cup champagne or white wine
¼ cup freshly grated Parmesan
  cheese

1. Preheat oven to 425°F.
2. Butter a baking dish, arrange oysters in dish, and sprinkle with chopped parsley and paprika.
3. Pour wine around oysters, and sprinkle with cheese.
4. Place in preheated oven 7 to 8 minutes, until well browned.
5. Serve at once.

PRAWNS WITH TARRAGON

If prawns are large, cut them in half. They will cook more quickly and will be easier to manage on the plate.
  When cleaning prawns, I like to leave on the tails for color and flavor.

2 tablespoons unsalted butter
2 teaspoons dried tarragon, or 2
  tablespoons chopped fresh
  tarragon
¾ pound prawns or scampi, shelled
  and cleaned
1 lemon
½ cup dry vermouth or white wine
½ cup heavy cream (optional)
Paprika

1. Melt butter in a sauté pan over medium heat, and stir in tarragon.
2. Add prawns and sauté for 1 minute.
3. Squeeze juice of lemon over prawns, add vermouth, and simmer 1 minute.
4. Add cream, and cook 3 minutes over high heat to reduce and thicken sauce.
5. Dust with paprika, and serve at once.

Variation:
Marinate prawns in mixture of melted butter, tarragon, lemon, and vermouth. Grill or broil 3 minutes on each side.

PRAWNS AND SCALLOPS

Eating well is one of the great pleasures of Genoa. The fresh fish is excellent and most often basil, the small-leaf variety, is the herb of choice.

12 prawns (6 ounces), shelled and cleaned
12 small sea scallops (6 ounces)
½ cup olive oil
1 teaspoon dried basil, or 1 tablespoon chopped fresh basil
2 lemons
3 cloves garlic
Freshly ground black pepper

1. Preheat broiler.
2. Place prawns and scallops in a shallow baking dish large enough to accommodate seafood in 1 layer.
3. Combine olive oil, basil, and juice of 1 lemon. Pour over prawns and scallops and turn in seasoned oil until they glisten on all sides.
4. Cut unpeeled garlic in half and add to dish.
5. Place dish on oven rack 3 to 4 inches from the source of heat. Broil seafood 2 minutes on each side, basting with sauce from pan. (Prawns will be pink, scallops very white.) Be careful not to overcook.
6. Season to taste with pepper, garnish with remaining lemon cut in half, and serve at once.

FILLETS OF SOLE

When I went into the fish market in Genoa, a pleasant briny odor came from the cases of fish. When fish is very fresh, it has the aroma of the incoming tide. This simple recipe is a perfect method for cooking fresh fish.

2 tablespoons unsalted butter
4 fillets of sole (¾ pound)
1 lemon
Freshly ground black pepper
1 lemon for garnish (optional)
1 tablespoon chopped parsley
  (optional)

1. Preheat oven to 500°F.
2. Place a shallow baking dish in the preheated oven until hot, about 2 minutes.
3. Remove dish from oven and put butter in dish to melt.
4. Put fillets in dish, turning them in the butter to coat both sides. Squeeze juice of 1 lemon over fish.
5. Place dish in oven and bake 3 to 4 minutes, until fish flakes when tested with a fork.
6. Season to taste with pepper.
7. Serve at once with Lemon-Mustard Butter (page 78), or simply garnish with lemon halves and parsley.

POACHED FISH

The port of Nice is lined on both sides with restaurants and cafés. In winter on a sunny day, it is possible to lunch outside. One afternoon we ate this well-flavored poached fish.

2 pieces halibut (¾ pound), or any white fish such as swordfish or red snapper, boned and skinned
2 lemons
4 cups water
6 peppercorns
½ cup white wine
2 sprigs parsley
1 bay leaf
1 scallion

1. Place fish on a plate and squeeze a few drops of lemon juice over it.
2. Place water in a sauté pan with peppercorns, wine, parsley, and bay leaf. Squeeze in remaining juice of 1 lemon, and place over high heat.
3. Slice scallion lengthwise into 2 thin strips, and add to pan.
4. When water comes to a boil, reduce heat to barely simmering. Add fish and poach until fish flakes easily when tested with a

fork in thickest area, about 5 to 6 minutes.

5. Arrange on a plate with remaining lemon cut in half, and serve with Watercress-Horseradish Sauce (page 78).

In Cannes I enjoy the atmosphere of the simple cafés and fish restaurants facing the flower market and fronted by baskets of oysters, mussels, shiny black sea urchins, and fat pink prawns. The grilled or broiled fish always seems especially appealing with its black marks from the grill.

2 slices tuna (¾ pound)
3 tablespoons olive oil
1 lemon
1 tablespoon fresh, grated ginger
¼ cup dry vermouth

1. Preheat broiler.
2. Place fish on a baking sheet.
3. Pour oil into a small bowl, and squeeze in juice of lemon. Add ginger and vermouth. Stir to combine well.
4. Coat both sides of fish with sauce. Place sheet on oven rack 3 to 4 inches from the source of heat.
5. Broil fish 3 to 4 minutes on each side, until golden, and baste with sauce while cooking. When done, fish will flake when tested with a fork.
6. Serve with Cucumber Sauce (page 79).

SWORDFISH
ITALIAN STYLE

When I think of fish, I think of a spring I spent in Elba. At the fish counters we would choose from the fishermen's night catch: a harvest of swordfish, cut into thick steaks to be grilled with rosemary; large prawns; sardines; mussels; clams; crabs; octopus; tuna; and a variety of delicate white fish.

2 tablespoons olive oil
1 clove garlic, peeled
½ teaspoon dried rosemary,
    or 2 teaspoons chopped fresh
    rosemary
1 tender stalk celery, cleaned
1 carrot, scraped
1 tomato, cleaned
½ cup dry white wine
1 piece swordfish (¾ pound), boned
    and skinned
Salt
Freshly ground black pepper

1. Warm oil in a sauté pan over medium heat. Add garlic, cut in half, and rosemary and stir.
2. Coarsely chop celery, carrot, and tomato; stir into pan, add wine, and simmer 3 minutes.
3. Cut swordfish into 3-by-3-inch pieces. Place in pan and cook over medium heat 5 to 6 minutes, until fish flakes when tested with a fork. Discard garlic.
4. Season to taste with salt and pepper, and serve at once.

BAKED SEA BASS

1 piece sea bass (¾ pound), boned
   and skinned
1 shallot, peeled
1 clove garlic, peeled
2 small dried red peppers
¼ cup olive oil
½ teaspoon dried oregano, or 2
   teaspoons chopped fresh oregano
½ teaspoon dried basil, or 2
   teaspoons chopped fresh basil
1 lemon
Freshly ground black pepper
1 tablespoon chopped parsley

1. Preheat oven to 425°F.
2. Place fish on a piece of foil or
   parchment paper, and set aside.
3. Chop shallot, garlic, and red
   peppers. Place in a bowl with oil,
   oregano, and basil. Squeeze in
   juice of lemon, and mix well.
4. Pour half of the sauce over the
   fish, and pinch foil together,
   leaving an opening across the
   top. Season to taste with pepper.
5. Place fish on a baking sheet and
   bake until fish tests done, about
   8 to 9 minutes.
6. Sprinkle with parsley, and serve
   at once with remaining sauce.

FILLETS OF SEA BASS WITH CAPERS

Other white fish, such as sole or
turbot, can also be used. Fennel is
good with this and other fish. It can
be served raw, cut in thin strips, and
dressed with olive oil and lemon
juice.

1 tablespoon flour
2 sea bass fillets (¾ pound), skinned
3 tablespoons unsalted butter
2 lemons
2 tablespoons capers, drained
1 tablespoon chopped parsley
¼ cup dry vermouth
Salt
Freshly ground black pepper

1. Sprinkle flour lightly over both
   sides of fillets.
2. Melt 2 tablespoons butter in a
   sauté pan over medium heat.
   When butter foams, add fish.
3. Cook fillets on both sides until
   golden brown and cooked
   through, about 4 to 5 minutes.
4. Squeeze juice of 1 lemon into
   pan. Add remaining 1 tablespoon
   butter, capers, parsley, and
   vermouth. Simmer 1 minute.
5. Season to taste with salt and
   pepper.
6. Serve fillets with remaining
   lemon cut in half or
   Lemon-Mustard Butter (page 78).

RED SNAPPER WITH ROQUEFORT SAUCE

4 tablespoons butter
1 bay leaf
2 red snapper fillets (¾ pound), boned and skinned
1 lemon
4 tablespoons soft Roquefort cheese
4 green olives with pimento in center, chopped
⅛ teaspoon cayenne pepper
¼ teaspoon paprika

1. Melt 2 tablespoons butter in a sauté pan over medium heat, add bay leaf, and place fish in pan.
2. Cut 2 thin slices from unpeeled lemon, and place 1 on each slice of fish.
3. Squeeze juice of remaining lemon over fish.
4. Cover pan and cook 4 to 5 minutes, until fish is white and opaque and flakes easily when tested with a fork.
5. Preheat broiler. Discard bay leaf. Combine remaining 2 tablespoons butter, cheese, olives, cayenne, and paprika. Cover fish with sauce and place under preheated broiler until sauce melts, about 1 minute.

SALMON WITH CAVIAR

This is a fast, yet impressive, dish for guests.

1 cup dry white wine
2 salmon fillets (¾ pound), skinned
1 tablespoon unsalted butter
½ cup heavy cream
One 2-ounce jar salmon or lumpfish caviar
Freshly ground black pepper

1. Pour 2 cups water into a sauté pan and add wine.
2. Place pan over high heat. When liquid comes to a boil, lower heat to simmer, and place salmon fillets in pan.
3. Use butter to coat a sheet of wax paper or parchment, and place over top of fish. Simmer salmon 4 to 5 minutes.
4. While salmon is poaching, pour cream into a small saucepan and place over high heat. Boil 2 to 3 minutes to reduce and thicken cream.
5. Stir in caviar and season to taste with pepper.
6. When salmon flakes easily when tested with a fork, remove from pan and place on a plate. Pour sauce over salmon and serve at once.

SALMON CAKES

Makes 8 cakes

One 7-ounce can salmon
1 shallot, peeled
4 sprigs parsley
1 egg
½ slice day-old bread
2 tablespoons oil
2 tablespoons unsalted butter
1 tablespoon flour
1 lemon

1. Drain salmon and place in blender or food processor. Add shallot and parsley sprigs, break in egg, add bread in small pieces, and blend well.
2. Warm 1 tablespoon each of oil and butter in a sauté pan over medium heat.
3. With a tablespoon, form salmon mixture into patties about ½ inch thick.
4. Sprinkle flour over cakes to lightly dust them.
5. Place cakes in pan and sauté until golden, about 2 minutes on each side. Add remaining oil and butter to pan as needed to make cakes.
6. Garnish with lemon cut in half, and serve with Watercress-Horseradish Sauce (page 78).

CRAB CAKES

Serve with thinly sliced raw cabbage tossed with vinaigrette sauce.

Makes 8 cakes

¾ cup cooked fresh crabmeat, or one 6-ounce can
½ lemon
1 egg
¼ cup dry bread crumbs
⅛ teaspoon red pepper
Tabasco
1 tablespoon flour
6 tablespoons safflower oil
2 tablespoons unsalted butter

1. Drain crabmeat and place in a bowl.
2. Squeeze juice of lemon half over crabmeat and stir.
3. Break egg into a bowl and beat for a few seconds until well blended.
4. Stir bread crumbs into bowl with egg; add red pepper and a few drops of Tabasco. Stir in crabmeat and combine well.
5. With a tablespoon, form mixture into small cakes. Dust lightly with flour on both sides.
6. Heat oil and butter in an 8-inch sauté pan over medium heat. Place 4 crab cakes at a time in pan and cook until brown and crisp, about 2 minutes on each side.

7. Place crab cakes on a warm plate and serve at once with Caper Sauce (following recipe).

CAPER SAUCE

Makes ½ cup

4 tablespoons olive oil
2 tablespoons red wine vinegar
10 parsley sprigs, stems removed
1 small shallot, peeled
1 tablespoon Dijon mustard
1 hard-boiled egg, peeled
2 tablespoons capers, drained

1. Place oil in a blender or food processor. Add vinegar and parsley, and purée.
2. Slice shallot into blender or food processor, and purée.
3. Add mustard. Slice egg into blender, and purée. Sauce will be thick.
4. Spoon sauce into a small bowl and stir in capers. Serve immediately.

CURRIED CRAB

In Barbados, we had a view from one restaurant of the water striped from jade to navy blue to indigo by the coral reefs, the sea washing the sand below, and tall hibiscus trees. We considered a lunch menu of lobster crêpes; yellowtail snapper; curried crab; and breadfruit and papaya seasoned with sugar, shaped into little balls, and deep-fried to a light crispness. We lingered over coffee until four in the afternoon.

2 scallions, washed
2 tablespoons unsalted butter
2 teaspoons curry powder
2 cups cooked crabmeat, canned, frozen, or fresh
¼ teaspoon cayenne pepper
2 limes
½ cup heavy cream or canned coconut milk

1. Finely chop scallions.
2. Melt butter in a sauté pan over medium heat, stir in scallions, and sauté until soft, about 2 minutes.
3. Stir in curry powder and cook 1 minute.
4. Add crabmeat and cayenne pepper, and squeeze in juice of limes. Sauté 1 minute.
5. Pour in cream or coconut milk and simmer over medium heat 2 minutes.
6. Serve at once on toast or a bed of rice.

SAUTEED SOFT-SHELL CRABS

Soft-shell crabs are sweet and succulent and best prepared simply.

1 tablespoon flour
4–6 medium-size soft-shell crabs
¼ cup sliced almonds
2 tablespoons butter
2 tablespoons oil
2 lemons

1. Preheat oven to 375°F.
2. Sprinkle flour over crabs to dust them lightly.
3. Spread almonds on a baking sheet and toast in oven until golden, about 3 minutes.
4. Melt butter and oil in a sauté pan over medium heat, and add crabs. Sauté until golden, about 3 minutes on each side.
5. Squeeze juice of 1 lemon over crabs, sprinkle with toasted almonds, and serve at once with remaining lemon cut in half.

SHAD ROE SAUTE

When properly cooked, the inside of this springtime delicacy is plump, tender, moist, and rich with flavor.

2 tablespoons unsalted butter
2 shad roes (½–¾ pound)
2 lemons
2 tablespoons chopped parsley
1 tablespoon capers
Freshly ground black pepper

1. Melt butter in a sauté pan over medium heat. Add roes and simmer slowly 4 to 5 minutes, being careful not to burn butter.
2. Turn as the roes become golden brown, and squeeze juice of 1 lemon over them.
3. Cover pan and cook 4 minutes.
4. Remove to a warm plate, sprinkle with parsley and capers, and season to taste with pepper.
5. Garnish with remaining lemon cut in half, and serve at once.

MUSSELS
IN SAFFRON SAUCE

The old quarter of Antibes contains possibly the best market along the whole coast, located beneath the walls of the Picasso Museum. Among the covered stalls are a feast of cheeses, all kinds of anchovy and sardine salads, and wine shops with a dozen different *rosés de Provence*. We tried a little restaurant behind a shellfish stall. The seafood was a revelation of freshness—wonderful shrimp fritters and small, sweet mussels.

24 mussels
2 cups dry white wine
1 clove garlic, peeled
¼ teaspoon saffron
1 cup heavy cream
1 tablespoon chopped parsley

1. Scrub mussels well, and place in a sauté pan with wine over medium heat.
2. Cut garlic in half, and add to pan.
3. Simmer 3 to 4 minutes, until mussels open. Remove mussels from shells and set aside.
4. Strain cooking liquid in a fine sieve, discard garlic, and return liquid to sauté pan. Stir in saffron and cream, and cook over high heat until sauce thickens, about 2 to 3 minutes.
5. Stir mussels into sauce, sprinkle with parsley, and serve at once.

SEAFOOD STEW

On a bright day we sat outside in a charming spot near Cannes. The geraniums and cyclamens were shining in the sunshine, the doves and pigeons cooing and fluttering, and the rich and fragrant fish stew was a masterpiece.

This recipe can be increased for parties. Serve with warm bread and a bottle of good red wine.

2 tablespoons olive oil
1 shallot, peeled
1 clove garlic, peeled
2 large tomatoes
1 bay leaf
1 teaspoon dried thyme
1 cup red wine
2 cups hot water
½ pound halibut, boned and skinned
¼ teaspoon cayenne pepper
6 clams, unshelled
10 prawns, unshelled
2 tablespoons chopped parsley

1. Warm oil in a saucepan over medium heat. Slice shallot, garlic, and tomatoes into pan. Add bay leaf and thyme, and sauté for 1 minute.
2. Add wine, then water, and boil 2 minutes over high heat.
3. Reduce heat to simmer, slice halibut into 4-inch strips, and place in pan. Add cayenne pepper and simmer 7 to 8 minutes, or until fish flakes.
4. Add clams and prawns in their shells and cook 3 to 4 minutes.
5. Place fish in soup bowls, and pour broth over fish.
6. Serve stew sprinkled with parsley.

LEMON-MUSTARD BUTTER

Makes about ⅓ cup

¼ cup unsalted butter, at room
  temperature
1 tablespoon Dijon mustard
Freshly ground black pepper
1 lemon

1. Place butter in a small bowl, and
   stir in mustard and pepper to
   taste.
2. Squeeze in juice of lemon, and
   mix well.

WATERCRESS-HORSERADISH SAUCE

Good with poached halibut, salmon,
or trout.

Makes about ½ cup

1 cup watercress leaves
½ cup sour cream
2 teaspoons prepared horseradish
2 teaspoons Dijon mustard
1 tablespoon fresh orange juice
Freshly ground black pepper

1. Place watercress leaves in blender
   or food processor and purée with
   sour cream.
2. Add horseradish, mustard, and
   orange juice. Blend well.
3. Place sauce in a bowl, and season
   to taste with pepper.

CUCUMBER SAUCE

English and Japanese cucumbers are crisp, and practically skinless, and have few seeds.

Makes about 1 cup

1 cucumber
½ cup olive oil
½ teaspoon dried thyme
1 teaspoon Dijon mustard
Cayenne pepper
1 lemon

1. With a sharp knife peel cucumber, leaving a few stripes of peel, and finely chop.
2. Pour oil into a small bowl. Add thyme, mustard, and a pinch of cayenne pepper.
3. Squeeze in juice of lemon, and stir in chopped cucumber.

Poultry

For quick cooking, chicken is a blessing. All parts can be quickly sautéed in butter or oil, and you can have a great meal in minutes.

Chicken is remarkably compatible with most herbs and spices: tarragon, rosemary, ginger, curry, and paprika. Chicken lends itself to brandy, red and white wine, vermouth, and Marsala, and is a good partner for most cheeses and vegetables, especially tomatoes, mushrooms, and artichoke hearts. Chicken has a natural affinity for lemons, limes, and oranges, and even combines well with fruits like grapes and apples.

In nearly every market you will be able to find chicken parts sold separately— breasts, legs, wings, thighs, livers—ideal for 1 or 2 people and for 15-minute meals. Remember:

- Try to buy fresh, not packaged, poultry. Chicken will spoil after a few days; refrigerate uncovered.
- Never salt poultry until the end of cooking.
- Chicken breasts, boned and skinned, cut into quarters, will cook quickly and be tender and full of flavor. Don't overcook, as they will toughen.
- Chicken legs and thighs, boned and skinned, then cut in half crosswise will cook more quickly and will be easier to handle than if left whole.
- Cook chicken thoroughly; raw chicken can be dangerous to your health.

PROVENCAL CHICKEN

Daily marketing is still the rule in Provence, where everything from cheese to chickens is sold to be eaten in a few hours, and everything is fresh. Young tender green peas are excellent with this dish.

2 chicken legs
2 chicken thighs
2 tablespoons olive oil
1 teaspoon dried basil, or 2 teaspoons chopped fresh basil
1 clove garlic, peeled
½ cup dry white wine
2 tomatoes
¼ cup pitted black olives
Salt
Freshly ground black pepper

1. Remove skin from legs and thighs.
2. Cut legs and thighs crosswise into 2 pieces each.
3. Warm oil in a sauté pan over medium heat. Stir in basil and garlic, cut in half. Add chicken, and brown about 3 minutes on each side.
4. Add white wine, slice tomatoes into pan, and add olives.
5. Cook, uncovered, over medium-high heat 10 minutes, until tender.
6. Season to taste with salt and pepper, and serve at once.

CHICKEN WITH BRANDY

1 whole chicken breast, boned and skinned
2 tablespoons unsalted butter
3 tablespoons brandy
8 mushrooms, cleaned
Salt
Freshly ground pepper
½ cup cream
Paprika

1. Cut breast in half and remove any fat.
2. Melt butter in a sauté pan over medium heat, add chicken, and cook until golden, about 3 minutes each side.
3. Add brandy to pan and simmer 3 minutes.
4. Slice mushrooms into pan and season with salt and pepper; simmer 3 minutes.
5. Add cream and simmer 3 minutes. Dust with paprika and serve from pan.

SAFFRON CHICKEN

Saffron adds a special touch to this dish.

2 chicken legs
2 chicken thighs
2 tablespoons butter
1 scallion
1 small dried red pepper
½ cup chicken broth
¼ teaspoon saffron
1 tablespoon curry powder

1. Remove skin from legs and thighs of chicken. Cut each piece in half crosswise.
2. Melt butter in a sauté pan over medium heat. Chop scallion and add to pan, sauté 1 minute until soft.
3. Add chicken and cook 2 to 3 minutes on each side, until golden brown.
4. Chop pepper very fine and stir into pan.
5. Combine broth, saffron, and curry powder; stir into pan.
6. Cover pan and cook 5 to 6 minutes. Serve at once.

CHICKEN WITH GRAPES

Rome is a feast for all the senses in any season. I had this ancient Roman dish in a rustic restaurant in Trastevere, the popular quarter of old Rome. This recipe is also suitable for Cornish game hens or squab. Quarter these small birds before sautéing.

1 whole chicken breast, boned and
   skinned
2 tablespoons unsalted butter
4 tablespoons brandy
1 cup seedless white grapes
½ cup dry white wine
Salt
Freshly ground black pepper

1. Cut breast in half, remove any fat.
2. Melt butter in a sauté pan over medium heat, add chicken and sauté until brown, about 4 minutes on each side.
3. Add brandy and touch with a lighted match.
4. When the flame goes out, stir in grapes and white wine. Simmer 5 to 6 minutes. Season with salt and pepper.
5. Serve chicken with grapes and sauce from pan.

CHICKEN WITH RED AND YELLOW PEPPERS, ROMAN STYLE

I had this wonderful chicken in an artist's studio in Rome within the old walls.

4–6 chicken thighs
2 tablespoons olive oil
1 small yellow bell pepper
1 small red bell pepper
1 ripe tomato
1 teaspoon dried rosemary, or 2
   teaspoons chopped fresh rosemary
1 clove garlic, peeled
½ cup dry white wine
Freshly ground black pepper

1. Remove skin from thighs. Cut each thigh into 2 pieces crosswise.
2. Warm oil in a sauté pan over medium heat. Place chicken in pan and sauté until golden brown, 3 to 4 minutes on each side.
3. Slice peppers, discarding seeds and ribs. Add to pan.
4. Slice tomato into pan, and stir in rosemary.
5. Chop garlic and add to pan. Pour in wine.
6. Cover pan and simmer 8 minutes over medium heat.
7. Season to taste with pepper, and serve at once.

CHICKEN TUSCAN STYLE

Serve this dish as the Florentines do, with a half lemon on each plate as a garnish.

1 chicken breast, boned and skinned
1 egg
¼ cup water
½ teaspoon dried sage
2 tablespoons flour
Salt
Paprika
¼ cup olive oil
1 lemon
2 sprigs parsley

1. Cut chicken breast in half, trim away any fat, and flatten halves to make as thin as possible.
2. Put egg in a small bowl with water and sage; mix with a fork to combine.
3. Dip chicken in egg mixture, one half breast at a time, dust lightly with flour, and then season with salt and paprika.
4. Heat oil in a sauté pan over medium heat. When oil is hot, sauté chicken 3 minutes on each side until golden brown.
5. Serve immediately with lemon halves and parsley garnish.

GINGER CHICKEN

1 whole chicken breast (¾–1 pound),
  boned and skinned
2 tablespoons soy sauce
½ cup white wine
1 clove garlic, peeled
1 tablespoon fresh grated ginger
2 tablespoons currant jelly
2 limes
1 tablespoon safflower oil
1 bunch watercress

1. Trim breast of any fat. Cut breast
   in half and then into quarters (4
   pieces).
2. To make the sauce, combine soy
   sauce and white wine in a small
   bowl. Slice garlic into bowl. Stir
   in ginger and currant jelly, and
   squeeze in juice of limes. Mix
   well.
3. Warm oil in a sauté pan over
   medium heat. Add breasts and
   cook 3 minutes on each side.
   Transfer to a plate.
4. Add sauce to sauté pan and boil
   over high heat 1 minute to
   reduce.
5. Return chicken to pan and cook
   1 minute, turning in sauce until
   nicely glazed.
6. Place on a bed of watercress, and
   serve hot or cold.

ROMAN CHICKEN

In Rome I enjoyed this dish with
Roman Cornbread (following recipe)
made with coarse cornmeal used for
polenta.

3 tablespoons olive oil
1 thick slice bacon, diced
1 clove garlic, peeled
1 teaspoon dried rosemary
1 teaspoon dried sage
6 chicken thighs, skin removed
2 ripe tomatoes, sliced
½ cup chicken broth or white wine
Salt
Freshly ground black pepper

1. Heat oil in a sauté pan over
   medium heat. Add bacon and
   garlic and sauté 1 to 2 minutes
   until soft, not brown.
2. Stir rosemary and sage into pan,
   add chicken, and cook until
   golden brown, about 3 minutes
   each side. Discard garlic.
3. Stir tomatoes into a separate pan;
   cover and cook over medium
   heat 2 to 3 minutes until soft.
   Rub through a sieve into pan
   with chicken.
4. Add chicken broth to pan and
   stir thoroughly to mix. Season
   with salt and pepper.

5. Cover pan and simmer 6 to 7 minutes. Serve immediately from pan.

ROMAN CORNBREAD

A thin, crisp cornbread.

Makes 15 squares

½ cup coarse cornmeal
½ cup water
1 egg
1 teaspoon baking powder
3 tablespoons flour
3 tablespoons melted butter

1. Preheat oven to 425°F.
2. Place cornmeal in blender or food processor. Add water, egg, baking powder, and flour; blend briefly, then add melted butter.
3. Butter a 9-by-6-inch pan. Pour mixture into pan and bake in preheated oven 10 minutes, until golden.
4. Serve at once.

POACHED
CHICKEN BREASTS

Simmered in rich broth, chicken breasts will be tender and moist. They can be served with a sauce made of their own broth (page 90), or as Oriental Chicken (page 91). As an added bonus, the cooked breasts can be refrigerated for 2 to 3 days.

3 cups chicken broth
2 whole chicken breasts, boned and skinned
2 medium-size carrots
2 scallions
8 sugar pea or snow pea pods
2 sprigs parsley
8 water chestnuts
4 red leaf lettuce leaves

1. Place broth in a saucepan over high heat.
2. Bring broth to boil and reduce heat to simmer.
3. Trim chicken breasts and cut in half to make 4 pieces. Add to broth and simmer slowly for 8 to 10 minutes, depending upon size. Don't boil or chicken will toughen.
4. Slice carrots and scallions lengthwise into long shreds and add to pan. Stir in peas, parsley, and water chestnuts.
5. When tender, remove chicken from broth to plate and wrap each piece of breast in a lettuce leaf. Discard bay leaf and reserve broth. Serve chicken breasts with vegetables and Sauce for Poached Chicken Breasts (following recipe).

SAUCE FOR POACHED CHICKEN BREASTS

Makes 1 cup

1 cup reserved chicken broth
(preceding recipe)
2 teaspoons Dijon mustard
2 tablespoons chopped parsley
Freshly ground pepper

1. Place broth in a small bowl.
2. Stir in mustard and parsley, and
   mix well. Season with pepper.
   Serve warm.

RED CRANBERRY SAUCE

Wonderful with turkey, chicken,
squab, and game hens.

Makes about ¾ cup

¼ cup red currant jelly
½ cup fresh orange juice
1 cup cranberries
2 tablespoons sugar
1 teaspoon grated orange rind

1. Place currant jelly in a small
   sauté pan over medium heat.
   Bring to a boil to melt jelly; add
   orange juice and simmer 3 to 4
   minutes.
2. Add cranberries; stir in sugar.
   Bring to boil, stirring as mixture
   thickens, 2 to 3 minutes.
3. Remove from heat and purée in
   blender or food processor.
4. Stir grated orange rind into
   purée. Serve cold, or at room
   temperature.

ORIENTAL CHICKEN

In summer this is a good solution for hot weather. Poach chicken in the morning as you prepare breakfast. Pour sauce over the chicken and refrigerate until evening. You will find this a fast and delicious dish for any season, if you make the sauce while the chicken is simmering.

2 Poached Chicken Breasts (page 89)
3 scallions
1 tablespoon soy sauce
1 tablespoon olive oil
1 tablespoon dry vermouth
1 tablespoon fresh grated ginger
Freshly ground black pepper

1. Cut chicken into slivers, and place in a bowl.
2. Slice scallions lengthwise into long strips, and place on chicken.
3. In a small bowl mix soy sauce, olive oil, vermouth, and ginger. Season with pepper.
4. Pour sauce over warm chicken breasts, so they can absorb the flavors.
5. Serve at room temperature on a bed of boiled rice.

ROAST QUAIL

In autumn the tables in Brussels are laden with pheasant, quail, partridge, creamy potato soups, and rich red wine. Serve with Cabbage Purée (page 61).

4 quail
Paprika
4 tablespoons soft unsalted butter
8 tablespoons yellow raisins or white grapes
4 strips bacon
4 slices white bread, crusts removed
4 sprigs watercress
1 lemon

1. Preheat oven to 450°F.
2. Cut each quail in half. Place quail in a baking dish; sprinkle paprika in each cavity.
3. Rub outside of birds with soft butter and paprika.
4. Place 1 tablespoon raisins in each cavity, and wrap each half with a half strip of bacon.
5. Place pan in preheated oven and roast birds 8 to 10 minutes, until tender.
6. Serve quail on buttered toast. Garnish with watercress and lemon quarters and serve at once with Orange-Ginger Sauce (following recipe).

ORANGE-GINGER SAUCE

Good with poultry and game,
especially roast quail.

Makes about ½ cup

½ cup red currant jelly
¼ cup fresh orange juice
1 teaspoon Dijon mustard
½ teaspoon powdered ginger
Pinch cayenne pepper

1. Place currant jelly in a small
   saucepan over medium heat; add
   orange juice and stir as jelly
   melts.
2. Stir in mustard, ginger, and
   cayenne, mixing well; allow to
   cook 1 minute. Put aside to cool.

SAUTEED SQUAB

Young squabs have pale rose or
bluish-white flesh. Avoid older
squabs, which can be tough. Serve
with Green Potatoes (page 37).

Two ¾-pound squabs
2 tablespoons unsalted butter
2 tablespoons cognac
8 small white mushrooms
1 slice cooked ham, ¼ inch thick
½ cup white wine
1 teaspoon paprika
¼ teaspoon powdered ginger
Freshly ground black pepper

1. Cut squabs into quarters.
2. Melt butter in a sauté pan over
   medium heat, and sauté squabs
   on all sides for 5 minutes.
3. Pour cognac over squabs and
   touch with a lighted match.
   When flame dies, cover pan and
   simmer for 3 minutes.
4. Chop mushrooms, cut ham in
   thin strips, add both to pan with
   squabs, and stir.
5. Add wine, paprika, and ginger
   and stir. Cover and simmer for 6
   minutes.
6. Season to taste with pepper, and
   serve at once with sauce from
   pan.

TURKEY FILLETS WITH CHEESE

2 thin turkey fillets (about 6 ounces each), from the breast
2 tablespoons unsalted butter
½ teaspoon dried sage
1 bay leaf
8 small white mushrooms
½ cup chicken broth
2 thin slices Fontina or Parmesan cheese
Freshly ground black pepper

1. Flatten turkey fillets by whacking them several times with the flat side of a chef's knife.
2. Melt butter in a sauté pan over medium heat, add sage and bay leaf. When butter foams, add turkey fillets. Cook them on both sides until golden, about 3 minutes each side.
3. Slice mushrooms into pan, add ¼ cup broth, and cook for 3 minutes. Discard bay leaf.
4. Place a thin slice of cheese on top of each fillet. Baste fillets with 1 tablespoon broth from pan. Cover pan and cook for 3 minutes. Add more broth as liquid evaporates.
5. Season to taste with pepper, and serve at once.

TURKEY FILLETS WITH MARSALA

I had this dish with Italian friends in a villa in Fiesole set amid the wooded hills overlooking Florence.

2 turkey fillets (about 6 ounces each), from the breast
2 tablespoons unsalted butter
1 teaspoon dried rosemary, or 2 teaspoons chopped fresh rosemary
2 tablespoons Marsala
4 tablespoons white wine or chicken broth
Freshly ground black pepper

1. Flatten the turkey fillets by whacking them several times with the flat side of a chef's knife.
2. Melt butter in a sauté pan over medium heat and add rosemary. When butter foams add turkey fillets. Cook on both sides until golden, about 3 minutes each side.
3. Add Marsala, and when it is bubbling add white wine. Cook 4 to 5 minutes, until tender.
4. Season to taste with pepper, and serve at once.

TURKEY FILLETS
WITH HAM

I was served this with *beignets* for dessert one evening in Arles. As we drove from the autoroute into Arles, the plane trees made a leafy green tunnel, framing acres of sunflowers, roses, grapevines, and cornstalks.

2 turkey fillets (about 6 ounces each), from the breast
2 tablespoons unsalted butter
1 bay leaf
2 tablespoons brandy
2 slices cooked ham (prosciutto), ¼ inch thick
½ cup dry white wine
¼ cup freshly grated Parmesan cheese
Freshly ground black pepper

1. Flatten turkey fillets by whacking them several times with the flat side of a chef's knife.
2. Melt butter in a sauté pan over medium heat. When butter foams, add bay leaf and turkey fillets. Cook them on both sides until golden, about 3 minutes each side.
3. Pour brandy over fillets and touch with a lighted match.
4. When flame dies, place 1 slice prosciutto on each fillet, pour in wine, and simmer for 3 to 4 minutes. Discard bay leaf.
5. Sprinkle on Parmesan cheese, cover pan, and cook for 1 to 2 minutes, until cheese melts.
6. Season to taste with pepper, and serve at once.

CHICKEN LIVERS
WITH SHALLOT SAUCE

The small shallot, with its papery skin and pale-pink color, adds a gentle flavor to dishes and sauces. The Florentines adore chicken livers and often serve *crostini* as an antipasto—thin slices of toasted bread spread with a smooth dark paste of chicken livers sharpened with anchovy.

2 tablespoons unsalted butter
1 teaspoon dried sage
¾ pound chicken livers
3 shallots, peeled
4 anchovies
¼ cup sweet vermouth
Freshly ground black pepper
1 tablespoon chopped parsley

1. Warm butter in a sauté pan over medium heat. Stir sage and livers into butter and sauté for 1 minute, until brown on the exterior but pink in center. Remove livers and reserve.
2. Chop shallots and place in pan. Sauté in butter 1 minute, until soft. Add anchovies and stir with shallots.
3. Pour vermouth into pan. Simmer over medium heat, stirring, 1 minute.
4. Add chicken livers to pan, and season to taste with pepper. Cook for 1 minute.
5. Sprinkle chopped parsley over the livers, and serve at once on toasted bread.

GRILLED CHICKEN WITH
SUMMER VEGETABLES

Select very fresh vegetables for grilling. One late summer day in Saint-Rémy in Provence we picked squash, peppers, and herbs in the garden and immediately grilled them with chicken.

1 chicken breast, boned and skinned
2 green zucchini
2 yellow squash
1 fennel bulb
1 red bell pepper
½ cup olive oil
2 teaspoons dried tarragon, thyme, sage, or basil
½ cup dry vermouth
2 garlic cloves, peeled, chopped
1 lemon
Freshly ground black pepper

1. Preheat broiler or outside grill.
2. Cut zucchini, squash, and fennel bulb into 1-inch-thick slices.
3. Quarter red pepper lengthwise, remove seeds and ribs.
4. In a bowl combine oil, tarragon, vermouth, and chopped garlic, and squeeze in juice of lemon. Toss vegetables and chicken in this mixture, place in an oven dish, and season with pepper.
5. Place dish on oven rack in preheated oven 3 to 4 inches from source of heat. Turn and baste with sauce until chicken and vegetables are tender, about 3 to 4 minutes on each side.

Meat

Here you will find a number of simple and fast ways to cook beef, veal, lamb, and pork.

Olive oil, garlic, and herbs are magical essences for flavoring meats: thyme and oregano add zest to beef; tarragon complements the subtlety of veal; rosemary enhances lamb; and sage is the herb of choice for pork.

Your sauces will have a highly individual quality when you season with fresh tomatoes, basil, or anchovies, and when oil or butter is the main cooking medium.

Vermouth adds glaze and shine to your sauces, while Marsala gives a distinctive taste of its own.

Here are some more suggestions for adding flavor to your meats:

- Trim meat carefully. Cook with a minimum of fat to prevent flare-ups and splattering. (Also, lean meat is better for your health.)
- Before grilling or broiling steak or lamb, cut a garlic clove in half and rub it over the meat.
- For pork or ham, wait until the meat is almost done and then grate lemon or orange peel over it; the oil in the peel adds perfume to the dish.
- Sprigs of rosemary, bay leaves, sage, and thyme are more potent when they have been sautéed in warm oil or butter for a few minutes before being added to the meat.
- Remember not to season meat with salt until the end of cooking, as salt draws out the juices.

ORIENTAL BEEF

Makes an appealing meal with plain rice or noodles.

1 fillet of beef (about ¾ pound)
2 tablespoons dry sherry
2 tablespoons soy sauce
2 tablespoons olive oil
1 clove garlic
1 shallot, peeled
1 small green or red bell pepper
4 mushrooms
1 tomato
Freshly ground black pepper

1. Carefully remove any fat from fillet. Thinly slice, and place on a plate.
2. Combine sherry and soy sauce, and pour over meat.
3. Warm oil in a sauté pan over medium heat. Cut unpeeled garlic in half, and place cut side down in oil to brown for a few seconds, then discard.
4. Slice shallot into pan, stirring 1 minute, until soft.
5. Cut pepper into 2-inch strips, discard seeds and ribs, and add to pan.
6. Add marinated beef and stir rapidly 1 minute.
7. Slice mushrooms and tomato into pan, cover, and cook 5 minutes.
8. Season to taste with pepper, and serve at once.

FILLET OF BEEF WITH VERMOUTH

1 tablespoon unsalted butter
2 fillets of beef (about 6 ounces each), ¾ inch thick
¼ cup sliced green olives
¼ cup dry vermouth
¼ cup heavy cream
Freshly ground black pepper

1. Melt butter in a sauté pan over medium heat. Add fillets and cook 2 to 3 minutes on each side.
2. Turn fillets when brown, and add olives.
3. Add vermouth and stir for 30 seconds.
4. Add cream and stir for 1 to 2 minutes, or until meat is done as desired.
5. Season to taste with pepper.
6. Arrange fillets on plates, pour sauce over them, and serve at once.

LAMB KEBABS

Kebabs offer savory and economical combinations of meat and vegetables and easy cooking.

4 tablespoons olive oil
1 lemon
1 cup white wine
1 teaspoon dried oregano
1 small eggplant
½ pound lamb cubes cut from leg
2 large sprigs of rosemary
10 small cherry tomatoes
Freshly ground black pepper

1. Preheat broiler.
2. Pour oil into a bowl and squeeze in juice of lemon. Add wine and oregano, and stir.
3. Cut unpeeled eggplant into cubes, and toss in sauce mixture.
4. Thread cubes of lamb on skewers, alternating with rosemary, tomatoes and eggplant. Place in a baking dish.
5. Pour remaining sauce over meat and vegetables, and place under preheated broiler about 3 inches from the source of heat.
6. Broil 5 to 6 minutes, turning skewers as lamb cooks.
7. Season to taste with pepper, and serve at once.

LAMB CHOPS WITH MUSTARD-HERB BUTTER

2 rib lamb chops, about 2 inches
  thick
1 clove garlic, peeled
½ lemon

1. Preheat broiler.
2. Carefully remove fat from chops.
3. Cut garlic clove in half. Rub
   chops on both sides with garlic.
4. Place chops in a baking pan, and
   squeeze juice of ½ lemon over
   them.
5. Place pan under preheated
   broiler 3 to 4 inches from source
   of heat and broil about 2 minutes
   on each side for pink chops.
6. Serve at once with a spoonful of
   Mustard-Herb Butter (following
   recipe) on each chop.

MUSTARD-HERB BUTTER

4 tablespoons unsalted butter, at
  room temperature
1 tablespoon Dijon mustard
½ lemon
1 teaspoon dried rosemary
1 teaspoon dried thyme
Freshly ground black pepper

1. Combine butter and mustard in
   bowl, and squeeze in lemon
   juice.
2. Stir in rosemary, thyme, and
   season to taste with pepper.

MEDALLIONS OF LAMB IN SWEET-AND-SOUR SAUCE

Makes a fast meal with sautéed vegetables.

2 loin lamb chops, about 2 inches thick
2 tablespoons butter
8 small mushrooms, cleaned
1 lemon
4 tablespoons red currant jelly
1 tablespoon red wine vinegar
1 tablespoon Worcestershire sauce
Freshly ground black pepper

1. Carefully remove fat and bone from chops.
2. Melt 1 tablespoon butter in a sauté pan over medium heat. When butter foams, add meat. Cook 1 minute on each side, until browned but rare inside. Transfer medallions to a plate.
3. Pour off excess fat from pan and add remaining tablespoon butter.
4. Thinly slice mushrooms into pan, sauté 1 minute, and squeeze in juice of lemon.
5. Mix together jelly, vinegar, and Worcestershire and stir into pan. Simmer over medium heat 1 minute.
6. Add medallions to pan, and simmer 1 minute more.
7. Season to taste with pepper, and serve at once.

LAMB CHOPS COOKED WITH TOMATOES

As we drove from Naples, we saw open trucks heavily laden with crimson tomatoes shining in the sun, bound for markets in Milan and Munich. Apulia's plateaus produce wheat, figs, grapes, olives, almonds, and tomatoes as they did in the Middle Ages. And the sea, blue-green and clear, is never far away.

2 loin lamb chops, about 1½ inches thick
2 tablespoons olive oil
1 tablespoon chopped fresh rosemary, or 2 teaspoons dried rosemary
2 ripe tomatoes, cut in half
Sea salt
Freshly ground black pepper

1. Carefully remove fat and bone from chops.
2. Heat oil in sauté pan over medium heat. Place lamb in hot oil.
3. Place unpeeled tomato halves into pan around lamb, and sprinkle rosemary over all.
4. Sauté chops until rare, about 2 minutes on each side, turning lamb and tomato halves as they brown.
5. Season to taste with salt and pepper, and serve at once.

LAMB PATTIES WITH RED AND YELLOW PEPPERS

In Provence in the summer, colors appear to be exaggerated—the red peppers, the yellow sunflowers seem too vivid to be real. Serve this with Spinach with Cheese (page 55).

½ pound ground lamb
1 lemon
1 small yellow onion, peeled
1 egg
2 tablespoons olive oil
2 teaspoons dried thyme
1 small red bell pepper
1 small yellow bell pepper
Freshly ground black pepper

1. Place lamb in food processor. Add juice of ½ lemon, and slice onion into processor. Add egg, and blend well.
2. Warm oil in a sauté pan over medium heat, add thyme, and stir for a few seconds.
3. Cut peppers into strips, discarding seeds and ribs. Place peppers in pan and stir until peppers become soft, about 2 minutes.
4. With a tablespoon, shape small patties of lamb mixture and flatten them with the back of the spoon.
5. Place lamb patties in hot oil with peppers and cook 2 to 3 minutes on each side, until golden and crusty.
6. Season to taste with black pepper.
7. Place patties and peppers on a warm plate, garnish with remaining ½ lemon cut into 2 pieces, and serve at once.

VEAL CHOPS WITH BASIL

I ordered this savory dish many times in a small neighborhood restaurant in Rome. Try it with a vegetable pasta.

2 rib veal chops, about ¾ inch thick
2 tablespoons olive oil
2 tablespoons chopped fresh basil, or
    1 tablespoon dried basil
2 tablespoons freshly grated
    Parmesan cheese
½ cup dry white wine
Freshly ground black pepper
1 lemon

1. Carefully remove any fat or gristle from chops.
2. Warm 1 tablespoon olive oil in a sauté pan over medium heat. Place chops in pan and cook about 2 minutes on each side, until golden.
3. While chops are cooking, place chopped basil in a small bowl and combine with 1 tablespoon olive oil and the grated cheese to make a paste.
4. When chops are turned, spread paste on browned side.
5. Add ¼ cup wine to bottom of pan, and season to taste with pepper. Stir and scrape bottom of pan.
6. Cover pan and simmer 5 to 6 minutes, until cheese is melted and chops are tender. Add more wine if liquid evaporates.
7. Place chops on warm plates, garnish with lemon halves, and serve at once.

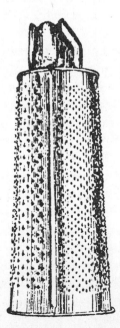

VEAL SCALLOPS WITH APPLES AND CALVADOS

In Brussels the cream is rich and thick. I had this luscious dish in a restaurant garden where wrought-iron chandeliers hung from chestnut trees.

6 thin veal scallops (½ pound)
3 tablespoons unsalted butter
1 medium-size green apple
3 tablespoons Calvados (or brandy)
½ cup heavy cream
Freshly ground black pepper

1. Carefully remove any fat and membrane from scallops.
2. Melt 2 tablespoons butter in a sauté pan over medium heat. When butter foams, sauté scallops 1 minute on each side, until golden. Transfer veal to a plate.
3. Pour off excess fat from pan, and add remaining butter. Thinly slice unpeeled apple into pan and cook in butter 1 minute, turning slices as they brown.
4. Stir in Calvados, scrape bottom of pan.
5. Pour cream into pan, raise heat to high, and rapidly boil 2 minutes to thicken cream. Stir cream constantly as it will quickly reduce.

6. Return veal to pan and cook 1 minute. Season to taste with pepper, and serve at once.

VEAL SCALLOPS WITH BLACK OLIVES

Serve with sliced tomatoes and Onion-Potato Purée (page 62).

6 thin veal scallops (½ pound)
2 tablespoons unsalted butter
1 lemon
½ cup dry white wine
¼ cup chopped black olives
Freshly ground black pepper

1. Carefully remove any fat or membrane from scallops.
2. Melt butter in a sauté pan over medium heat. When butter foams, sauté scallops until golden, 1 minute on each side.
3. Squeeze juice of lemon over veal, add white wine to pan, and simmer 2 minutes, stirring bottom of pan.
4. Stir olives into pan and simmer 2 minutes. Season to taste with pepper, and serve at once.

CRISP VEAL CAKES

These are good with a bowl of Escarole Soup (page 19).

1 lemon
½ pound ground veal
1 egg
1 teaspoon dried oregano
2 anchovies
2 tablespoons olive oil
Freshly ground black pepper
3 tablespoons sweet vermouth
1 tablespoon capers

1. Grate rind of lemon and set aside.
2. Place ground veal in food processor with egg, oregano, and anchovies. Squeeze juice of lemon into mixture, and combine.
3. With a tablespoon, make small cakes of veal and flatten with back of spoon.
4. Heat oil in a sauté pan over medium heat and place veal in hot oil. Allow cakes to cook 3 to 4 minutes on each side, until golden and crusty.
5. Sprinkle lemon rind over cakes while they are cooking, and season to taste with pepper.
6. Place cakes on warm plates, pour vermouth into pan, and stir quickly over high heat for a few

seconds, loosening the brown bits clinging to the pan.

7. Pour sauce from pan over the veal, garnish with capers, and serve at once.

VEAL KIDNEYS SAUTE

Try this kidney dish with braised endive and a bottle of red wine.

4 veal kidneys (¾ pound)
2 tablespoons unsalted butter
1 shallot, peeled
2 tablespoons brandy
¼ cup dry vermouth
1 teaspoon Dijon mustard
Freshly ground black pepper
1 lemon
4 pieces bacon (optional)

1. Cut kidneys lengthwise, remove fat cores, and cut crosswise into ¼-inch slices.
2. Melt butter in sauté pan over medium heat. Slice shallot into pan, and sauté 1 minute, until soft.
3. Add kidney slices and sauté until golden brown, about 1 minute on each side.
4. Pour in brandy, ignite it, and shake the pan until flames go out. Transfer kidneys to a plate.
5. Pour out excess fat, add vermouth, and stir over medium heat to collect all the brown bits from pan.
6. Add mustard and pepper to taste, and squeeze in juice of lemon.

7. Return kidneys to pan, baste with sauce, and cook 1 minute.
8. Serve at once with crisp bacon.

PORK CHOPS WITH RED WINE

Good with Braised Celery (page 57).

2 center-cut loin pork chops, about
   1-inch thick
1 clove garlic, peeled
½ onion, peeled
2 mushrooms, cleaned
1 carrot, scraped
1 tablespoon olive oil
¼ cup chicken broth
Salt
Freshly ground black pepper
1 bay leaf
¼–½ cup red wine

1. Remove fat and bone from chops.
2. In a blender or food processor combine and purée garlic, onion, mushrooms, and carrot.
3. Heat oil in a sauté pan over medium heat, add pork, and cook until golden brown, about 2 minutes on each side. Remove and put aside.
4. Pour oil out of pan, add vegetables and broth. Place pork on a bed of vegetables, season with salt and pepper, and add bay leaf.
5. Add ¼ cup wine to pan, cover and simmer 7 to 8 minutes, until pork is tender and cooked through. Add more wine, if needed.
6. Serve at once with vegetables and sauce from pan.

PORK CHOPS WITH FENNEL

In Brussels the endives and fennel are eaten just out of the earth.

4 center-cut loin pork chops, about 1 inch thick
1 tablespoon unsalted butter
1 small fennel bulb
½ cup chicken broth
1 tablespoon fennel seeds
2 tablespoons Pernod
Salt
Freshly ground black pepper

1. Carefully remove fat and bone from chops; use only the lean, thick loin from the center.
2. Melt butter in a sauté pan over medium heat. When butter foams, place pork in pan and cook 2 minutes on each side, until golden brown.
3. While pork is cooking, chop the fennel coarsely.
4. Remove pork and pour excess fat from pan.
5. Add chicken broth to pan and stir to deglaze. Place pork in center of pan and surround with fennel and fennel seeds. Cover pan and cook over medium heat 8 to 9 minutes, until pork is cooked through.
6. Add Pernod, and cook 2 minutes.
7. Season to taste with salt and pepper, and serve at once.

PORK CHOPS WITH PRUNES

Serve with Turnips with Chives (page 60).

4 rib pork chops, about ½ inch thick
2 tablespoons olive oil
1 teaspoon sage
½ onion, peeled
Salt
Freshly ground black pepper
8 canned prunes
1 bay leaf
½ cup sweet white wine

1. Carefully remove fat from chops.
2. Heat 1 tablespoon oil in a sauté pan over medium heat, and add sage. Place chops in hot oil and cook until golden brown, about 2 minutes each side. Remove and put aside.
3. Pour oil out of pan, add remaining 1 tablespoon oil, slice onion into pan and quickly sauté 1 minute. Season with salt and pepper.
4. Place prunes in pan, add chops, bay leaf, and white wine. Cover pan, and simmer 7 to 8 minutes, until pork is tender and cooked through.
5. Remove bay leaf, and serve at once from pan.

PORK CHOPS PAPRIKA

I found this recipe in northern Italy, where veal or pork is often cooked in milk or cream. The onion melts into the lovely pale-pink, creamy sauce. You will find this a perfect dish with small steamed potatoes and green beans.

2–4 pork loin chops, about 1¼ inches thick
2 teaspoons unsalted butter
1 small yellow onion, peeled
½ teaspoon paprika
1 cup heavy cream
1 teaspoon capers
1 tablespoon chopped parsley

1. Carefully remove fat and bone from chops; use only the lean, thick meat from the center.
2. Melt butter in a sauté pan over medium heat. When butter foams, place pork in pan and cook about 2 minutes on each side, until golden brown.
3. Remove pork, and pour excess fat from pan.
4. Slice onion into pan, stir, and add paprika and cream.
5. Add pork, cover pan, and simmer over medium heat 7 minutes.
6. Remove cover from pan, raise heat to high, and rapidly boil 2 minutes to thicken and reduce cream.
7. Garnish with a light dusting of paprika, and serve at once with capers and parsley sprinkled over.

HAM SLICE WITH SHERRY-APRICOT GLAZE

Pick up a slice of ham at the delicatessen on your way home; with Golden Biscuits (page 8) and a green salad, this makes a fast and pleasing meal.

1 slice ham, 1 inch thick
1 tablespoon unsalted butter
6 canned or fresh apricots
2 tablespoons honey
1 orange
2 tablespoons grated orange peel
2 tablespoons chopped parsley
1 tablespoon sherry

1. Carefully trim all fat from ham.
2. Melt butter in a sauté pan over medium heat. When butter foams, place ham in pan and arrange apricots around it.
3. In a bowl mix together honey, juice of orange, grated orange peel, parsley, and sherry.
4. Baste ham slice and apricots with mixture as ham cooks, about 4 minutes each side.
5. Serve at once.

HAM FRITTERS

The salty-sweet taste of the ham is accented with Horseradish Sauce (following recipe).

Makes 8 fritters

1 slice ham, ¼ inch thick
1 egg
¼ cup milk
2 tablespoons flour
2 teaspoons Dijon mustard
Cayenne pepper
2 tablespoons olive oil
Freshly ground black pepper

1. Trim fat from ham and discard. Cut ham into pieces, put in food processor, and finely mince.
2. Break in egg, add milk, flour, mustard, and a few grains of cayenne, and blend with ham to make a thick purée.
3. Heat oil in a sauté pan over medium heat. Place spoonfuls of ham mixture in hot oil and flatten with back of spoon.
4. Cook fritters, turning once as they become golden, about 2 minutes each side.
5. Season to taste with pepper, and serve at once.

HORSERADISH SAUCE

Makes about 1 cup

½ cup heavy cream
2 tablespoons prepared horseradish
4 tablespoons mayonnaise
1 teaspoon Dijon mustard
2 teaspoons red wine vinegar

1. Place cream in a bowl and whip until stiff.
2. Fold in horseradish, mayonnaise, mustard, and vinegar, and mix well.

One-Dish Meals

When your energy is low, the weather is bad, guests arrive at the last minute, or you are in a do-nothing mood, one-dish meals can be easily assembled and cooked. It is your good fortune, when circumstances demand, to be able to put a meal together quickly. The meal can be cooked in one pan, served from one pan, and when you return to the kitchen after dinner is over, there is just one pan to wash!

Some of the following meals can be made with what you have on your shelf. Even the most discriminating cooks occasionally look for the easy way out, and you will find that resourceful and pleasing meals are, indeed, possible from one dish.

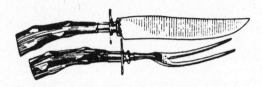

CHICKEN WITH ARTICHOKE HEARTS

A friend in Paris has a large houseboat anchored by the Pont Neuf, the oldest bridge in Paris, built during the reign of Henry IV. We often had this one-dish meal as his boat traveled slowly up the Seine.

1 whole chicken breast (¾ pound), boned and skinned
2 tablespoons unsalted butter
½ cup dry sherry
4 artichoke hearts, cooked
6 large mushrooms
½ cup heavy cream
Freshly ground black pepper

1. Cut breast into 4 pieces.
2. Melt butter in a sauté pan over medium heat. When butter foams, add breasts and brown on all sides. Add sherry, cover, and cook for 5 minutes.
3. Slice artichoke hearts and mushrooms. Add to pan with chicken, and cook, uncovered, 2 to 3 minutes.
4. Pour cream into pan, bring to a boil, and stir, scraping bottom of pan. Simmer 2 to 3 minutes, until sauce thickens.
5. Season to taste with pepper, and serve at once from pan.

CHICKEN WITH HERBS

4 chicken thighs
2 tablespoons olive oil
1 teaspoon dried basil
1 teaspoon dried thyme
1 teaspoon dried oregano
1 small yellow onion, peeled
2 tomatoes
1 cup chicken broth
½ pound wide noodles (tagliatelle)
Freshly ground black pepper

1. Remove skin from chicken and cut each thigh in half crosswise.
2. Warm oil in a sauté pan over medium heat, add basil, thyme, and oregano.
3. Add chicken and sauté until golden, about 3 minutes on each side.
4. Slice and coarsely chop onion, and add to pan.
5. Slice unpeeled tomatoes into pan, add broth and simmer 3 to 4 minutes.
6. Place noodles in a large pot of rapidly boiling water and cook 3 to 4 minutes. Drain.
7. Add noodles to pan with chicken. Cover pan and simmer 3 minutes.
8. Season to taste with pepper, and serve at once from pan.

STUFFED LETTUCE LEAVES

6 large lettuce leaves, iceberg lettuce
1 clove garlic, peeled
8 mushrooms, cleaned
1 cup ground cooked ham, lamb, or
   veal
¼ cup chopped parsley
¼ cup bread crumbs
¼ cup freshly grated Parmesan
   cheese
1 egg
3 tablespoons butter
½ cup chicken broth
Salt
Freshly ground black pepper

1. Wash lettuce leaves well, and dry.
   Spread on a flat surface.
2. Chop garlic and mushrooms and
   place in a bowl with ham,
   parsley, bread crumbs, and
   cheese. Stir egg with a fork and
   add to mixture.
3. Put 1 to 2 tablespoons stuffing
   on each leaf and make fat rolls.
4. Melt butter in a heavy skillet,
   place lettuce rolls side by side.
   Add broth and season with salt
   and pepper.
5. Cover pan and simmer over
   medium heat 10 minutes. Serve
   with broth from pan.

CHICKEN LIVER PILAF

A fondly recalled Roman meal.

2 cups chicken broth
½ cup Arborio rice
½ pound fresh peas
1 tablespoon unsalted butter
1 tablespoon olive oil
½ pound chicken livers
2 tablespoons pine nuts
2 tablespoons currants
Freshly ground black pepper

1. Pour broth into a saucepan and
   bring to boil over high heat.
2. Stir rice into saucepan, reduce
   heat to simmer, and cook 7 to 8
   minutes.
3. Shell peas into small bowl and
   reserve.
4. Warm butter and oil in a sauté
   pan over medium heat. Slice
   livers in half, add to pan, and
   sauté about 1 minute, until
   brown on the exterior but pink in
   center. Reserve livers and juices.
5. Add peas to rice, and stir.
6. Taste rice and when nearly
   tender, add livers and juices from
   pan, pine nuts, and currants and
   cook 1 to 2 minutes longer, until
   rice is done.
7. Season to taste with pepper, and
   serve from pan at once.

VEAL WITH ZUCCHINI

A simple, delicious Florentine dish.

2 tablespoons unsalted butter
1 tablespoon olive oil
2 shallots, peeled
1 teaspoon dried thyme
4 zucchini
½ pound thinly sliced veal scallops
¼ cup chicken broth
Salt
Freshly ground black pepper
1 tablespoon chopped parsley

1. Warm 1 tablespoon butter and oil in a sauté pan over medium heat. Chop shallots and stir into pan. Add thyme.
2. Slice zucchini into pan and sauté vegetables together over medium heat 2 minutes. Remove vegetables and put aside.
3. Add remaining tablespoon butter to pan, add veal, and sauté 2 minutes, turning as scallops brown.
4. Add broth to pan and stir to catch all bits from bottom of pan. Add vegetables, season with salt and pepper, and cook 2 minutes.
5. Sprinkle with chopped parsley and serve from pan.

PORK WITH CABBAGE

A sweet-and-sour dish.

2 center-cut loin pork chops, 1 inch thick
2 tablespoons unsalted butter
½ small white cabbage
1 large white potato
1 tablespoon red currant jelly
¼ cup red wine vinegar
½ cup water
Paprika
2 tablespoons sour cream

1. Carefully trim bone and fat from chops.
2. Melt butter in a sauté pan over medium heat. Add chops and cook about 2 minutes on each side, turning as chops brown.
3. Finely slice cabbage and potato and stir into pan.
4. Combine jelly, vinegar, and water in a small pan over medium heat, stirring until hot. Pour over meat and vegetables.
5. Cover pan and simmer 7 to 8 minutes, until cabbage and potatoes are cooked.
6. Dust with paprika, and serve at once from pan with a tablespoon of sour cream on each plate.

LIMA BEANS WITH SAUSAGES

This is a savory Florentine bean stew. Add a bottle of red wine and good bread.

4 mildly flavored Italian sausages
1 cup dry white wine
1 large ripe tomato
1 cup canned small lima beans, drained
½ teaspoon dried thyme
2 tablespoons chopped parsley
Freshly ground black pepper

1. Cut each sausage into 3 pieces.
2. Place a sauté pan over medium-high heat. Add sausages and ½ cup wine. Simmer 2 minutes to drain fat from sausages.
3. Pour off wine and fat from sausages. Slice tomato into pan, and add remaining ½ cup wine. Cover pan and cook over medium heat 7 minutes.
4. Place beans in a bowl. Stir thyme and chopped parsley into beans.
5. Stir bean mixture into pan with sausages, and cook, uncovered, 3 minutes.
6. Season to taste with pepper, and serve from pan at once.

CRAB AND SHRIMP WITH RICE

2 cups chicken broth
2 tablespoons unsalted butter
1 clove garlic
½ cup brown rice
4 large mushrooms
1 tomato
½ cup small shrimp, cleaned
½ cup crabmeat, canned or fresh
1 tablespoon chopped parsley
Freshly ground black pepper

1. Pour broth into a saucepan and simmer.
2. Melt butter in a sauté pan over medium heat. Cut unpeeled garlic in half, and place cut side down in butter. Sauté garlic until golden, then discard.
3. Stir rice into pan and add 1 cup broth.
4. Slice mushrooms and tomato into pan.
5. Simmer over medium-high heat 7 to 8 minutes. When broth is absorbed, add more. (Finished dish should not be liquidy.)
6. Stir shrimp and crabmeat into rice and cook 2 minutes.
7. Stir parsley into rice, season to taste with pepper, and serve at once from pan.

PAN BAGNA

This is truly a one-dish meal. I first had this spicy sandwich for lunch in a marketplace in Provence. There, if you don't make it to market by nine, the ripest, most beautiful of the fruits and vegetables are gone.

2 eggs
½ cup olive oil
1 teaspoon dried oregano
Freshly ground black pepper
2 tablespoons red wine vinegar
One 7-ounce can Italian tuna, packed
  in oil
6 anchovy fillets, chopped
¼ cup black olives, chopped
2 large round hard rolls
1 ripe tomato
4 romaine lettuce leaves

1. Put eggs in a saucepan and cover with water. Place over medium heat and simmer 6 minutes. Plunge into cold water.
2. Pour oil into a small bowl. Add oregano, pepper to taste, and vinegar, and stir. Mix in tuna with oil from can, and stir well. Add anchovy fillets and olives.
3. Cut rolls in half horizontally and place on a plate. Put 2 tablespoons tuna-vinaigrette mixture on each top half.
4. On bottom halves of rolls place a slice of tomato and a lettuce leaf. Shell and slice eggs into thin rounds. Place egg slices on top of lettuce.
5. Pour remaining tuna-vinaigrette mixture over each bottom. Cover with top halves of rolls and serve at once.

Salads and Dressings

A salad by its very nature is a mixture of things, and the possibilities are infinite. There are hot salads and refreshing cold salads, fruit salads, salads composed of green and leafy vegetables, some made of only chopped vegetables, some of sweet and savory ingredients. The Italians serve numerous kinds of cooked vegetables, dressed with oil and lemon, that are also salads.

A salad is an ingenious way to include vegetables and necessary nutrients in your menu. Salads have always appealed to dieters because of their low calorie count, and their crisp freshness can be enjoyed all year round.

Salads are the most movable of feasts; they can be served at the beginning, during, or at the end of the meal, or they can be a main course.

Generally, salads fall into three categories:

1. A few tender young greens dressed with vinaigrette, served as an accompaniment to richer, heavier foods.
2. A variety of vegetables, chopped or sliced, cooked or raw, with vinaigrette, served as an hors d'oeuvre at the beginning of a meal.
3. Vegetables, eggs, poultry, meat, fish, cheese, pasta, or rice combined with greens, oil and vinegar, lemon juice and cream, or mayonnaise, served as a main dish for a simple meal.

More than any other food, salads demand proper care and attention and a light hand. The greens and other ingredients should be selected with thought for color, taste, and texture. Try to find seasonal greens for your salads.

There are many types of lettuce in the markets. The following are the most common: small heads of crisp limestone; tender butter or Boston lettuce; dark-green romaine; escarole, with slightly bitter feathery leaves; ivory-colored Belgian endive; tart watercress or arugula; magenta radicchio.

A great variety of greens and vegetables can be eaten raw and are used to make salads: cabbage, spinach, fennel, celery, celery root (celeriac), sprouts, bell peppers, and radishes, to name only a few.

DRESSING THE SALAD

When dressing the salad, oil and vinegar, like seasonings, are a matter of taste and preference.

For most salads a fine olive oil is best. Olive oil can be made from any of about fifty different varieties of olives, so there is a wide range of flavors, odors, and colors, depending upon the variety, where the olives are grown, and how the oil is extracted and processed. Some olive oils are more suited to cooking, others for use in salads, and still others for sauces and marinades. Extra-virgin olive oils, which have the most distinctive flavors, are made from the first pressings of top-quality olives (some are hand-pressed). Virgin olive oil is not always made with top-quality olives. Pure olive oil, the lowest grade, can be made from second or third pressings of the same olives used to make virgin oil.

Fine vinegars, in all their various colors and tastes, play a great part in salads and in cooking. Red or white wine vinegar or lemon juice is usually used in making dressings. Good vinegar is aged, like wine. For example, the mature, amber balsamic vinegar imparts a distinctive soft quality to salads and vegetables that a younger vinegar does not. All vinegars can be flavored by infusion: add some sprigs of fresh herbs—tarragon, rosemary, basil—to a good white wine vinegar and soon it will be ready to perfume salads.

The following are suggestions for successful salads:

- The greens must be carefully washed and dried. They should be thoroughly rinsed with cold water and drained well in a colander.
- To store greens, wrap them in paper towels or a muslin towel and store them in the vegetable compartment of the refrigerator. Cared for properly, greens will keep for several days.
- Always toss salad just before serving. The delicate leaves should be mixed well with dressing, but not bruised or crushed.
- Salads taste best cool, not cold straight from the refrigerator.
- The tender inner leaves of greens are preferable to the leathery outer leaves.
- When using garlic, rub the surface of a stale piece of bread or toast with the cut end of an unpeeled clove; place the bread in the salad bowl, toss with the greens, and remove the bread before serving. (One should never find garlic pieces in the salad.)

- Tarragon, parsley, thyme, chives, and other fresh herbs add zest to a salad. Dried herbs are good, too.
- Freshly ground pepper is another element that contributes to the success of a salad dressing.
- When using salt, sea salt is a nice addition to a salad; it lends texture as well as flavor.

VINAIGRETTE

Makes ½ cup

There is nothing better than a plain green salad made with a variety of fresh tender lettuces, seasoned with pure olive oil, a good wine vinegar or the juice of a lemon, seasonings, and herbs. The classic recipe for vinaigrette is one-third vinegar and two-thirds oil.

6 tablespoons olive oil
2 tablespoons vinegar or lemon juice
Dash of salt
Freshly ground black pepper to taste

1. Pour oil into a bowl and mix with any seasonings and condiments you desire.
2. Then add the vinegar or lemon juice.

HERB VINAIGRETTE

Fresh herbs contribute color and texture as well as distinctive flavors to salads.

Makes about ⅔ cup

⅓ cup olive oil
1 teaspoon Dijon mustard
1 teaspoon chopped parsley
2 teaspoons chopped fresh basil, or 1 teaspoon dried basil or tarragon
2 teaspoons chopped fresh thyme, or 1 teaspoon dried thyme
1 tablespoon wine vinegar
1 lemon
Dash of salt
Freshly ground black pepper to taste

1. Pour oil into a bowl, and stir in mustard, parsley, basil, and thyme to mix.
2. Add vinegar and stir.
3. Squeeze in juice of lemon, add salt and pepper, and mix to blend.

BASIC
BLENDER MAYONNAISE

Mayonnaise is one of the most versatile of all sauces. Flavored with lemon juice, wine, or fruit juice, it makes a very thin binding for vegetable, fish, meat, and fruit salads. Coarsely chopped vegetables, meat, or fish can be tossed with mayonnaise in advance so they absorb its flavor.

The amount of oil used in a mayonnaise recipe varies, depending upon the type of oil (heavy or light) and the size of the eggs.

Makes about 1½ cups

1 egg, at room temperature
½–¾ cup olive oil or salad oil, or
   combination of both
1 lemon
1 teaspoon Dijon mustard
Sea salt
Freshly ground black pepper

1. Break egg into blender and process.
2. With blender running, add oil in a thin stream until egg and oil thicken and do not separate.
3. Squeeze in juice of lemon, add mustard, season to taste with salt and pepper, and blend to combine.

CREAMY MAYONNAISE

Makes about 2 cups

1½ cups Basic Blender Mayonnaise
   (preceding recipe)
¼ cup whipped cream
¼ cup sour cream
1–2 tablespoons fresh lemon juice
1 teaspoon Dijon mustard
Freshly ground black pepper

1. Place mayonnaise in a bowl; stir in whipped cream and sour cream.
2. Add lemon juice and stir well to blend thoroughly.
3. Stir in mustard and season to taste with pepper.

ORANGE MAYONNAISE

Makes about 2 cups

Good with fruit salads, ham, and cold chicken.

1½ cups Basic Blender Mayonnaise (page 126)
½ cup fresh orange juice
1 tablespoon chutney
⅛ teaspoon cayenne pepper
¼ teaspoon powdered ginger
2 teaspoons grated orange rind

1. Place mayonnaise in a bowl, stir in orange juice slowly, and blend well.
2. Add chutney, cayenne, and ginger and stir well.
3. Add grated orange rind and stir until thoroughly blended.

MAYONNAISE WITH HERBS

Makes about 2 cups

Good with fish, vegetables, and cold meats.

1½ cups Basic Blender Mayonnaise (page 126)
½ cup watercress leaves, chopped
1 teaspoon chives, chopped
1 tablespoon chopped fresh parsley and tarragon, combined
2 teaspoons fresh lemon juice
⅛ teaspoon cayenne pepper
Freshly ground black pepper

1. Place mayonnaise in a bowl; stir in watercress, chives, and mixed herbs.
2. Add juice and cayenne, and season to taste with black pepper.

SEAFOOD MAYONNAISE

Serve with cold crab, prawns, or
lobster.

Makes about 1 cup

1 egg yolk, at room temperature
½ cup oil
1 lemon
1 tablespoon Dijon mustard
2 tablespoons white rum
1 tablespoon tomato catsup
Freshly ground black pepper

1. Place egg yolk in blender, turn
   on motor, and pour in the oil
   very slowly.
2. Blend until yolk and oil thicken
   and do not separate. Squeeze in
   juice of lemon, add mustard, and
   blend.
3. Add rum and catsup, and blend
   to combine.
4. Pour dressing into a small bowl,
   and season to taste with pepper.

MIXED GREEN SALAD

In northern Italy I am struck by the
complexity of the salads, the diversity
of colors, shapes, flavors, and
textures. The young leaves of spinach
make a good raw salad; the older
leaves are best cooked or made into
soups.

1 head soft lettuce, such as Boston or
   red leaf, washed and dried
10–12 young spinach leaves, washed
   and dried
½ fennel bulb, or 3 inner stalks
   celery, washed and dried
½ cup olive oil
1 teaspoon Dijon mustard
Sea salt
Freshly ground black pepper
1 lemon
¼ cup dry white wine

1. Place the soft lettuce leaves in
   the bottom of a salad bowl.
   Remove spinach stems, and cut
   leaves into long, thin strips. Add
   them to bowl.
2. Cut fennel or celery into thin
   slices, and add to bowl.
3. Combine oil, mustard, salt, and
   pepper to taste, and mix.
   Squeeze in juice of lemon, and
   add wine.

4. Just before serving, pour
   dressing over salad and toss
   gently.

ENDIVE SALAD

A light dressing heightens the subtle
flavors of the endives, mushrooms,
and apple.

2 Belgian endives, washed and dried
4 mushrooms, cleaned
1 apple, peeled
4 tablespoons Basic Blender
   Mayonnaise (page 126)
Salt
Freshly ground black pepper
1 lemon
1 tablespoon balsamic vinegar
2 tablespoons chopped almonds

1. Slice endives lengthwise into a
   salad bowl.
2. Coarsely chop mushrooms and
   apple, and add to bowl.
3. In a small bowl combine and mix
   mayonnaise, salt, pepper, juice of
   lemon and vinegar.
4. Pour dressing into salad bowl,
   add almonds, and toss gently.
   Serve this salad cold.

ENDIVE AND ORANGE SALAD

One autumn day I had lunch with friends in Naples in a hotel that stands at the very edge of a cliff overhanging the sea. We stopped for an apéritif in a tiny bar, then went into the dining room. It had a delicately painted vaulted ceiling and windows to the floor, creating a light-flooded room. We were seated with a view of the terrace and the water far below. And the food! This salad was fantastic.

2 endives
1 orange
1 bunch watercress, washed and
   dried (or curly endive)
⅓ cup olive oil
Sea salt
Freshly ground black pepper
½ cup orange juice
1 tablespoon balsamic vinegar

1. Slice endives lengthwise into a salad bowl.
2. Peel the orange and thinly slice it crosswise into bowl. Add watercress leaves, discarding stems.
3. Pour oil into a small bowl, season to taste with salt and pepper, and mix. Add orange juice and vinegar, and stir to blend.
4. Pour dressing over salad, toss gently, and serve.

ROMAINE AND ROQUEFORT SALAD

I have had this salad often in France; the leaves of romaine are a crisp contrast for the creamy, strong-flavored cheese.

1 head romaine lettuce, washed and
   dried
⅓ cup olive oil
3 tablespoons heavy cream
3 tablespoons Roquefort cheese
1 tablespoon red wine vinegar
Freshly ground black pepper

1. Discarding the outer leaves, slice romaine in half lengthwise. Place each half on a salad plate.
2. Pour oil into a bowl, add cream, and mix.
3. With a fork, mash Roquefort cheese, and stir into oil. Add vinegar, and stir to combine.
4. Pour dressing over romaine, and season to taste with pepper.

RADICCHIO SALAD

Radicchio can be found in markets all over Italy and now in most local markets here. The city of Treviso, north of Venice, claims radicchio as its own and every December celebrates with a radicchio fair. Try radicchio dressed lightly with olive oil and balsamic vinegar, and sprinkled lightly with freshly grated Parmesan cheese. The handsome red leaves add a colorful and appetizing touch to salads.

15 stems arugula, washed and dried
1 small head radicchio, washed and
    dried
⅓ cup olive oil
Sea salt
Freshly ground black pepper
2 tablespoons fresh lemon juice
1–2 teaspoons balsamic vinegar
¼ pound piece Romano or Parmesan
    cheese

1. Place arugula leaves in a salad bowl, discarding tough stems.
2. Tear radicchio leaves into pieces and add to bowl.
3. Pour oil into a small bowl; season to taste with salt and pepper and stir. Add lemon juice and vinegar and mix well.
4. With a vegetable peeler, cut thin slivers of cheese.

5. Just before serving, add cheese, pour dressing over salad, and toss.

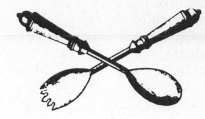

TOMATOES WITH GORGONZOLA

2 ripe red tomatoes
2 ripe yellow tomatoes, or 2
  additional red tomatoes
⅓ cup olive oil
¼ cup fresh basil, chopped
¼ pound imported Gorgonzola
  cheese
Freshly ground black pepper
2 tablespoons pine nuts, toasted

1. Slice tomatoes and arrange on a
   platter.
2. Drizzle half of the olive oil over
   tomatoes.
3. Scatter basil over tomatoes, and
   add the remaining oil.
4. Crumble the Gorgonzola and
   sprinkle over slices; season to
   taste with pepper.
5. Scatter pine nuts over slices, and
   serve.

PRAWN AND MELON SALAD

1 small cantaloupe
½ pound prawns, cleaned, cooked
1 cup Orange Mayonnaise (page 127)
4 tablespoons sour cream
Freshly ground black pepper
1 head butter lettuce, washed and
  dried
2 tablespoons fresh tarragon or
  chives, chopped

1. Peel and seed cantaloupe and cut
   into cubes. Place with prawns in
   a salad bowl.
2. In a small bowl, combine
   mayonnaise, sour cream, and
   pepper to taste. Spoon into bowl
   with prawns and melon and mix
   well.
3. Arrange lettuce leaves around
   sides of salad bowl; add
   prawn-and-melon mixture and
   sprinkle salad with chopped
   herbs.
4. Refrigerate until ready to serve.

WHITE BEAN SALAD

One 15-ounce can white beans,
  drained
½ cup olive oil
Sea salt
Freshly ground black pepper
3 tablespoons red wine vinegar
2 small ripe tomatoes
1 small red onion
10 whole oil-cured black olives, pitted

1. Rinse beans with warm water,
   and place in a salad bowl.
2. Pour oil into a small bowl,
   season to taste with salt and
   pepper, and mix. Add vinegar
   and stir.
3. Pour dressing over beans and
   toss well.
4. Thinly slice tomatoes and red
   onion into bowl with beans.
5. Add olives and toss gently.

WATERCRESS AND POTATO SALAD

You can use small new potatoes in a
variety of combinations in your
salads: with string beans and peas,
radicchio, or chopped herbs. When
using potatoes or rice in a salad,
marinate with the dressing while hot.

10–12 very small new red potatoes,
  unpeeled
½ cup dry white wine
⅓ cup olive oil
1 teaspoon Dijon mustard
Sea salt
Freshly ground black pepper
1 tablespoon lemon juice
1 bunch watercress, washed and
  dried

1. Place potatoes in a sauté pan,
   add water to cover, and boil 5 to
   6 minutes, until tender. Drain
   potatoes.
2. When cool enough to handle,
   slice potatoes into a bowl, and
   pour white wine over them.
3. Pour oil into a small bowl, stir in
   mustard and lemon juice and
   season to taste with salt and
   pepper. Stir dressing well.
4. Pour dressing over potatoes, add
   watercress leaves, discarding
   stems, and toss gently.
5. Serve at room temperature.

GREEN BEANS WITH BASIL

I recall a lovely meal in Provence with friends: local rosé wine; fresh green bean salad with basil, a touch of cream, and black olives; a gratin made of layers of sliced tomatoes, potatoes, herbs, garlic, and oil.

½ pound small green beans
4–6 small inner stalks celery
2 tablespoons heavy cream
2 tablespoons chopped fresh basil or parsley
4 tablespoons chopped black olives
Sea salt
Freshly ground black pepper
1 lemon

1. Place 2 cups water in a sauté pan over high heat.
2. Break beans in half, and place in boiling water. Cook 3 to 4 minutes, until crisp but tender.
3. Drain beans, reserving ¼ cup cooking liquid. Place beans in a salad bowl.
4. Cut celery into 1-inch pieces, and add to bowl.
5. In a small bowl, mix cream, reserved cooking liquid, basil, and olives. Season to taste with salt and pepper. Squeeze in juice of lemon, and stir well.
6. Pour dressing over celery and beans and toss gently.
7. Serve at room temperature.

PAPAYA AND SHRIMP SALAD

½ pound tiny shrimp, cleaned and cooked
3 limes
1 tablespoon grated fresh ginger
4 tablespoons Creamy Mayonnaise (page 126)
1 papaya, peeled, cut in half, seeds removed
¼ teaspoon paprika

1. In a bowl mix shrimp with juice of 2 limes; add ginger and mayonnaise.
2. Squeeze juice of remaining lime over both halves of papaya. Pile shrimp mixture into papaya. Season with paprika.
3. Chill in refrigerator until ready to use.

GREEK RICE SALAD

Greek Rice Salad combines lots of parsley with crunchy radishes. In summer this makes a meal with warm bread and dessert.

2 cups water
½ cup Arborio rice
⅓ cup olive oil
Sea salt
Freshly ground black pepper
2 lemons
1 tablespoon balsamic vinegar
10 radishes
¼ cup chopped parsley

1. Place water in a sauté pan over high heat. When water boils, add rice and simmer about 8 to 9 minutes, until al dente.
2. Pour oil into a bowl, and season to taste with salt and pepper. Squeeze in juice of lemons, add vinegar, and stir well.
3. As soon as rice is tender, stir into bowl with dressing and mix.
4. Slice radishes very thin into bowl. Add parsley and toss gently.
5. Serve at room temperature.

SHRIMP SALAD WITH TOMATOES AND CAPERS

This is a substantial salad. Try it with a light main dish for a quick meal.

2 heads soft lettuce, such as Boston or butter, washed and dried
¼ pound cooked shrimp
¾ cup mayonnaise
1 tablespoon cognac
2 tablespoons chopped parsley
2 tablespoons capers
1 small tomato
Sea salt
Freshly ground black pepper

1. Line a salad bowl with a few large lettuce leaves. Add inner small leaves and hearts of lettuce.
2. In a small bowl, combine shrimp, mayonnaise, cognac, parsley, and capers.
3. Coarsely chop tomato and force through a sieve into mayonnaise mixture. Season to taste with salt and pepper.
4. Pour sauce with shrimp into salad bowl, and toss salad lightly. Serve immediately.

FRESH TUNA SALAD

A wonderful combination of flavors.

2 tablespoons red wine vinegar
2 slices fresh tuna (½ pound), boned
  and skinned
¼ cup olive oil
1 tablespoon fresh lemon juice
1 tablespoon mayonnaise
2 tablespoons capers, drained
Freshly ground black pepper
1 bunch arugula or watercress,
  washed and drained
½ red onion, peeled and sliced thin

1. Place 2 cups water in a sauté
   pan; add 1 tablespoon vinegar
   and bring to boil; reduce heat to
   simmer, and add tuna.
2. Simmer tuna 3 to 5 minutes,
   until tender; remove from water
   and set aside to cool.
3. Pour oil into a bowl; add lemon
   juice, mayonnaise, and remaining
   tablespoon of vinegar. Stir well,
   until thoroughly blended and
   creamy.
4. Add capers to dressing, reserving
   a few for garnish; season to taste
   with pepper.
5. Arrange crisp arugula or
   watercress on a flat shallow dish;
   with a tablespoon, spoon
   dressing over arugula. Place
   onion slices on arugula and

spoon dressing over; add tuna
and spoon dressing over; sprinkle
reserved capers over top and
serve.

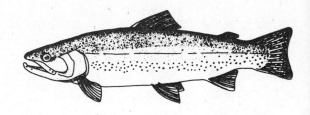

Desserts

Aren't we all tempted by creamy cakes, lemon tarts, sweet sauces, pale ices, and rich ice creams? Who is not enticed by the scent and color of sun-ripened peaches and summer berries? Mixed with whipped cream, they are even more tantalizing.

A dessert can be whatever suits the season and the meal: a pungent cheese, a bunch of grapes, an almond wafer to dunk in a glass of sweet wine, or a chocolate mousse. A meal can be ended on a simple note with a red apple and cheese or with the grand flourish of a flaming sauce.

There are many happy surprises here for those who are looking to find easy and imaginative endings for their meals.

MACEDOINE OF SUMMER FRUITS

One of our pleasant chores on Elba was shopping for food in Portoferraio's markets. We would go early to get the best of the ripe red and yellow peppers, tomatoes, zucchini, cherries, peaches, plums, grapes, and nectarines.

2 plums, 2 apricots, or 2 peaches (or any combination you like)
1 cup blackberries or blueberries
2 oranges
1 small bunch seedless grapes
6–7 fresh mint leaves
½ cup white wine or leftover champagne
½ cup plain yogurt
2 tablespoons honey

1. Cut plums, apricots, or peaches in half, remove stones, and place in a bowl. Add blackberries.
2. Remove skin of 1 orange and slice fruit thinly into bowl.
3. Remove grapes from stems and place in bowl. Add fresh mint leaves.
4. Pour wine over fruit, and squeeze in juice of 1 orange.
5. Place yogurt in a small bowl, stir in honey, and mix well to make a sauce.
6. Serve fruit with sauce.

WINTER FRUIT DESSERT

A very simple winter dessert that can be made when fresh fruit cannot be found. It is delicious, and very impressive. Peaches may also be used for this dessert.

¼ cup red currant jelly, or plum jam
¼ cup red Burgundy wine
1 tablespoon sugar
½ lemon
6 canned plums, drained of syrup
¼ cup brandy

1. Place jelly and wine in a saucepan over medium heat, stir to dissolve jelly. Add sugar and squeeze in juice of lemon.
2. When jelly is dissolved and mixture is simmering, spoon plums into mixture and heat them thoroughly.
3. Heat a serving spoon, then pour a small amount of the brandy into the spoon; ignite and pour, flaming, into the plums and sauce.
4. Immediately pour rest of brandy into the plums, stir and baste plums until flame subsides. Serve plums with sauce alone, or with vanilla ice cream with sauce over all.

STRAWBERRIES WITH RASPBERRY SAUCE

Served with vanilla ice cream, this is heavenly.

1 pint strawberries
1 orange
2 tablespoons sugar
2 tablespoons water
½ pint raspberries

1. Place strawberries in a colander, wash and hull them, and slice into a bowl. Squeeze in juice of orange.
2. Place a small saucepan over medium heat, add sugar and water, and heat to boiling. Stir in raspberries and cook over low heat for 5 to 6 minutes.
3. Place raspberries in blender and purée.
4. Drain strawberries. Pour raspberry sauce over them and serve.

Variation:
Fill Quick Crêpes (page 10) with raspberry sauce and dust with sugar.

ZABAIONE

This versatile Italian dessert can be made in advance, served warm or as a frozen dessert, and may be served as a sauce for a platter of assorted fresh fruits.

1 whole egg
2 egg yolks
¼ cup sugar
2 tablespoons Marsala or white wine

1. Break egg into a nonmetal bowl, add egg yolks and sugar, and beat with a rotary beater or whisk for a few minutes, until mixture is thick and creamy. Add Marsala or wine.
2. Place bowl inside a saucepan with hot water halfway up its sides. Place saucepan over medium heat. When water starts to simmer, beat 2 to 3 minutes, until mixture is pale yellow, light, and fluffy. Be careful not to overcook.
3. Remove bowl from water and pour into glasses. Serve hot or cold, with cookies or on sponge cake.

Variation:
For sauce to serve over fresh fruit, whip 1 cup heavy cream until thick and fold into cool zabaione.

POACHED FRESH FIGS

This poaching method can also be used with plums, apricots, and peaches.

½ cup water
½ cup sugar
4–6 fresh figs (or plums, apricots, or peaches)
2 tablespoons brandy

1. Put water and sugar in a saucepan and bring to boil over high heat. Simmer for 4 minutes.
2. Place unpeeled figs in syrup and simmer for 4 minutes.
3. Warm brandy and pour over figs, ignite, and let flame burn out.
4. Serve with a Zabaione Sauce made with whipped cream (preceding recipe) or Raspberry Sauce (page 140).

APPLES WITH CRANBERRIES

A very pretty dessert that is also very low in calories.

2 Golden Delicious apples, medium size (or pears)
½ cup fresh orange juice
½ cup fresh cranberries

1. Peel and slice apples (remove and discard cores), and place in a sauté pan.
2. Put orange juice in pan with apples and bring to boil over high heat; reduce to simmer and cook 3 to 4 minutes, basting with a tablespoon.
3. Stir cranberries into pan and cook for a few minutes; when first berry pops, they are done.
4. Serve in a bowl, cool or at room temperature, with juices.

PEACHES
WITH CARAMEL SAUCE

Very good with almond macaroons.

2 peaches
1 lemon
4 tablespoons sugar
2 tablespoons water
½ cup heavy cream
½ cup chopped almonds

1. Peel peaches and cut in half, removing pits. Place halves in a bowl, and squeeze juice of lemon over them.
2. In a small saucepan, combine sugar and water. Cook over high heat, stirring constantly, until mixture turns a deep brown, about 2 minutes.
3. Pour in cream, bring to a boil, and cook until sauce is smooth, about 1 to 2 minutes.
4. Place 2 peach halves on each plate, spoon caramel sauce over peaches, and sprinkle with almonds.

Variation:
Plums may be poached and then covered with caramel sauce.

GLAZED BANANAS

This simple dessert will delight your guests. It's delicious on its own, but for a special treat, serve it with Apricot Sauce (following recipe).

3 firm bananas
1 tablespoon unsalted butter
½ cup fresh orange juice
¼ cup Grand Marnier
4 macaroons, crumbled
¼ cup almonds, chopped

1. Peel bananas and slice in half lengthwise.
2. Melt butter in a sauté pan and add bananas.
3. Mix orange juice with Grand Marnier and pour into sauté pan. Simmer bananas over medium heat 8 to 10 minutes, basting until soft.
4. Sprinkle crumbled macaroons over bananas and add chopped almonds: baste several times with sauce in pan.
5. Serve at room temperature.

APRICOT SAUCE

Makes ½ cup

½ cup apricot jam
1 orange
2 tablespoons Grand Marnier

1. Place apricot jam in a small saucepan, and squeeze in juice of orange.
2. Place over medium heat and simmer until sauce bubbles, about 2 minutes.
3. Stir in Grand Marnier.

POACHED PEARS WITH CHOCOLATE SAUCE

Use the best chocolate you can find for this simple but luscious dessert.

2 cups water
½ cup white wine
2 tablespoons sugar
1 lemon
1 Anjou pear
1 cup fresh or frozen raspberries

1. Place water, wine, sugar, and a few drops of lemon juice in a saucepan. Place over medium heat, and simmer 2 to 3 minutes.
2. Peel pear and cut in half; remove core, making cavities a bit larger with a sharp knife.
3. Add pear to simmering liquid and cook, covered, 4 to 5 minutes.
4. Remove pear from pan with a slotted spoon and set aside to cool; allow liquid to continue to boil to reduce.
5. Fill pear cavity with Chocolate Sauce (following recipe).
6. Place raspberries in blender or food processor and purée until smooth; add ¼ cup poaching liquid to purée.
7. Before serving, spoon raspberry sauce onto the plates; place half pear in center of each plate and spoon sauce over pear. Serve cool or at room temperature.

CHOCOLATE SAUCE

3 ounces semisweet chocolate
½ cup heavy cream

1. Break chocolate into a small bowl.
2. Place 2 cups water in a sauté pan over medium heat. Place bowl in pan to melt chocolate.
3. When chocolate is melted, stir in cream and simmer 1 minute.

APPLE FOOL

Makes an easy but splendid dessert by itself or with Apricot Sauce (page 143).

2 Golden Delicious apples
1 orange
½ cup water
½ cup heavy cream
2 tablespoons confectioners' sugar

1. Slice unpeeled apples into a saucepan, and place over medium heat.
2. Using a sharp knife, cut 2 thin strips of orange peel (zest only) and add to pan. Squeeze in juice of orange, and add water.
3. Bring liquid to boil and simmer 4 to 5 minutes, until apples are tender.
4. Place apples, orange zest, and liquid in blender or food processor and purée.
5. Pour cream into a bowl and whip until cream holds soft peaks.
6. Add sugar and fold in apple purée.

Variation:
Make Quick Crêpes (page 10) and fill with Apple Fool. Warm ¼ cup brandy or Cointreau, pour over filled crêpes, and ignite.

RICH CHOCOLATE DESSERT

I found this chocolate delight in Paris in a Proustian tea salon where they melt chocolate bars to make their hot chocolate.

3 ounces milk chocolate
2 tablespoons water
2 egg yolks
¼ cup heavy cream
2 teaspoons instant coffee
¼ cup chopped almonds

1. Put 3 cups water in a saucepan, place over medium heat and simmer.
2. Break chocolate into a bowl, and add 2 tablespoons water. Place bowl in water in pan to melt chocolate.
3. In a separate bowl, beat egg yolks with a whisk, add cream, and stir in coffee.
4. Stir egg-yolk mixture into melted chocolate and keep it over hot water, stirring constantly until mixture is thick and smooth, about 2 minutes.
5. Stir in almonds.
6. Pour into 2 individual serving dishes, and refrigerate until ready to serve.

SESAME SEED WAFERS

Genoa has some of the prettiest sweetshops, cafés, and bars that I have ever seen. Like those of Venice and Vienna, they are decorated with crystal and gilt. We enjoyed this unusual wafer in a small café.

Makes about 16 wafers

3 tablespoons unsalted butter, at room temperature
⅓ cup brown sugar
1 egg
½ cup flour
½ teaspoon vanilla
¼ cup sesame seeds or pine nuts

1. Preheat oven to 400°F.
2. Place butter in a food processor or blender and combine with brown sugar. Break egg into food processor or blender, add flour and vanilla, and blend well.
3. Stir in sesame seeds.
4. Drop small teaspoons of mixture onto a buttered baking sheet, leaving space for wafers to spread.
5. Place in preheated oven to bake 6 to 7 minutes, until wafers spread and have lacy brown edges. They will be very thin.

HAZELNUT THINS

One late afternoon we went to a fishing village near Genoa. There we ate ices and munched on hazelnut cookies as we watched the sun go down.

Makes 24 cookies

1 egg
½ cup brown sugar
3 tablespoons unsalted butter
1 teaspoon vanilla
⅓ cup flour
½ cup hazelnuts

1. Preheat oven to 400°F.
2. Break egg into food processor. Mix for a few seconds, then add sugar, butter, and vanilla.
3. Add flour and blend.
4. Add hazelnuts and blend for a few seconds, until nuts are coarsely chopped.
5. Drop batter by teaspoonfuls onto a buttered baking sheet, leaving plenty of space between rounds, as the batter will spread.
6. Place in preheated oven and bake 3 to 4 minutes.

ALMOND COOKIES

The markets of the Marais in Paris offer epicurean delights. Narrow side streets harbor specialties from around the world: almonds, cumin, dried cod, coffee, vanilla beans, saffron, rare spices, and a limitless assortment of candied fruits cut in large chunks for cakes and desserts.

Makes 12 small cookies

½ cup almonds
2 tablespoons unsalted butter
¼ cup sugar
1 tablespoon flour
2 tablespoons milk
1 teaspoon almond or vanilla extract

1. Preheat oven to 375°F.
2. Place almonds in food processor or blender and grind fine.
3. Add butter and sugar and blend with almonds.
4. Add flour, milk, and almond or vanilla extract and mix well.
5. Drop batter by teaspoonfuls in small rounds onto a buttered baking sheet.
6. Place in preheated oven and bake 4 to 5 minutes.

ORANGE-HONEY COOKIES

In Morocco the perfume of orange blossoms is overpowering in the still, warm air. Oriental carpets were laid under the trees for a picnic in the shade. We were offered hot mint tea in glasses and small cookies made of honey.

Makes 8 cookies

3 tablespoons unsalted butter
½ cup flour
1 teaspoon baking powder
2 tablespoons orange juice or orange flower water
2 tablespoons honey

1. Preheat oven to 400°F.
2. Place butter, flour, and baking powder in food processor and blend.
3. Add orange juice and honey and mix to combine.
4. Place teaspoonfuls of batter on a buttered baking sheet.
5. Place in preheated oven and bake 6 to 7 minutes, until lightly colored.

RAISIN WAFERS

There is a popular café in the Piazza della Signoria where, in winter, older Florentines drink warm white wine with sugar and eat these crisp wafers.

Makes 24 wafers

1 egg
4 tablespoons unsalted butter
2 tablespoons sugar
1 cup flour
1 teaspoon lemon juice
½ cup raisins

1. Preheat oven to 400°F.
2. Break egg into food processor and blend with butter, sugar, flour, and lemon juice.
3. Stir in raisins.
4. Place ball of dough on an ungreased baking sheet. Roll out dough to ⅛ inch thickness, and cut into 1½-by-3-inch strips.
5. Place in preheated oven and bake 6 to 7 minutes.

OAT COOKIES

I found these cookies in London.
They are irresistible.

Makes 8 large cookies

3 tablespoons unsalted butter
½ cup flour
1 teaspoon baking powder
½ cup brown sugar
1 teaspoon vanilla
2 tablespoons milk
½ cup oats

1. Preheat oven to 400°F.
2. Place butter in food processor and blend with flour and baking powder.
3. Add brown sugar, vanilla, and milk. Mix to blend, and stir in oats.
4. Place heaping teaspoonfuls of batter on an ungreased baking sheet.
5. Place in preheated oven to bake 6 to 7 minutes. Be careful not to overcook, as cookies bake quickly.

RICH CHOCOLATE COOKIES

Makes 24 cookies

½ cup unsalted butter
⅓ cup sugar
1 egg
¼ cup cocoa
¼ cup flour
1 teaspoon vanilla

1. Preheat oven to 400°F.
2. Combine butter and sugar in a food processor, add egg, cocoa, flour, and vanilla, and mix.
3. Drop by teaspoonfuls onto a buttered baking sheet. Place in preheated oven and bake 2 to 3 minutes. Watch carefully, as cookies burn easily.
4. Remove immediately from baking sheet and cool on a rack.

CARROT-ORANGE CAKE

Makes 12 squares

3 tablespoons unsalted butter
2 carrots
½ cup brown sugar
1 egg
1 cup flour
1 teaspoon baking powder
Grated rind of 1 orange
1 tablespoon orange juice
⅓ cup dark raisins
1 cup heavy cream
2 tablespoons confectioners' sugar
2 tablespoons dark rum

1. Preheat oven to 400°F.
2. Place butter in a 9-by-6-inch baking pan, and put pan in oven to melt butter.
3. Grate carrots in a food processor. Add brown sugar, egg, and melted butter from pan and blend.
4. Combine flour and baking powder; add ½ cup to ingredients in processor and mix, then add remaining half and mix. Add grated orange rind and orange juice, and blend. Stir in raisins.
5. Put in buttered pan, place in preheated oven and bake 10 to 12 minutes, until top is golden.
6. Pour cream into a bowl and whip until it holds soft peaks. Stir in sugar and rum.
7. Serve cake with flavored whipped cream.

GINGER CAKE

This is a delicate, fine-textured cake that is as light as air. Sprinkle with candied ginger, or frost cake in the pan with Lemon Icing (following recipe).

Makes 10 squares

1 egg
3 tablespoons unsalted butter
½ cup sugar
1 cup flour
1 teaspoon baking powder
2 teaspoons powdered ginger
¼ cup sour cream
1 lemon
2 tablespoons chopped candied
  ginger

1. Preheat oven to 375°F.
2. Break egg into food processor, add butter and sugar, and blend.
3. In a separate bowl, combine flour, baking powder, and ginger. Add slowly to food processor and mix well.
4. Add sour cream, squeeze in juice of lemon, and blend.
5. Place batter in a buttered 9-by-6-inch baking pan and bake in preheated oven 10 to 12 minutes, until top is golden and sides shrink from pan.
6. Sprinkle candied ginger over cake while warm.

LEMON ICING

1 tablespoon unsalted butter
4 tablespoons confectioners' sugar
1 lemon

1. Put butter in a small bowl, add 3 tablespoons sugar, and blend.
2. Add 1 tablespoon lemon juice and stir. If icing is not firm enough, add a bit more sugar, but it should be a thin glaze.

WHITE CHOCOLATE SQUARES

Makes 12 squares

3 tablespoons unsalted butter
⅓ cup sugar
1 egg
3 ounces white chocolate
1 scant cup flour
1 teaspoon baking soda
¼ cup sour milk or buttermilk
1 teaspoon vanilla

1. Preheat oven to 375°F.
2. Place butter, sugar, and egg in food processor. Mix until smooth and creamy.
3. Break chocolate into a small bowl and place bowl in simmering water over medium heat to melt chocolate.
4. Combine flour and baking soda, and add one-half to mixture in food processor.
5. Pour milk into food processor and mix. Add remaining flour and combine well.
6. Add vanilla and melted chocolate to mixture, and combine well.
7. Spoon batter into a buttered 9-by-6-inch baking pan, and bake in preheated oven 9 to 10 minutes, until top is golden and sides shrink from pan. A moist cake, be careful not to overcook.

Entertaining &
Seasonal Menus

Entertaining means getting together with friends. Arranging a party is putting together the people, the food, the table, and trying to create an occasion everyone will enjoy, including you.

Make your entertaining easier with a relaxed spirit of hospitality. Allow your guests to share in the activity and preparations, so you will have more time to be with them. Make it possible for them to circulate freely, to cluster and move around a table with bottles and glasses where they can mix their drinks, toss a salad, season a sauce, chop, peel, stir, or taste. Plates can be filled right from the stove, then everyone can move to a table set with candles, flowers, and wine. A relaxed party encourages laughter and interesting talk.

Fresh fruits and vegetables give endless inspiration for table or buffet decorations. Avoid an ambitious menu; food is not meant to impress but to be enjoyed. Please your guests with a few dishes that are well cooked. It is far better to be relaxed and in control than to be overwhelmed by a meal that is too much work at the last minute.

Keep the menu pared down and the food simple, especially after a full day's work. Remember, the shopping, washing, and putting away take extra energy. If you plan to do some of the preparation and cooking in advance, you will feel less anxiety and will feel more secure. Always buy seasonal foods of the best quality. You should decide the menu when you go to market, according to what looks good to you.

Here are some ideas for meals that lend themselves well to comfortable entertaining.

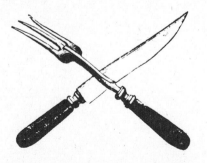

SPRING MENUS

Spring means Paris in April or May. The gardens in the Tuilleries, the gardens lining the Champs-Elysées, the Luxembourg Gardens, all ablaze with the color of blooming flowers and budding green trees.

Asparagus Custard
Poached Fish with Red-Pepper Sauce
Braised Lettuce
Almond Cookies

Pork Chops with Fennel
Italian Potatoes with Sage
Green Beans with Basil
Strawberries with Raspberry Sauce

Garlic Soup
Golden Biscuits
Fresh Tuna Salad
Peaches with Caramel Sauce

Tiny Baked Tomatoes with Mustard
  Sauce
Shad Roe Sauté
Mixed Green Salad
Poached Pears with Chocolate Sauce

Lamb Patties with Red and Yellow
  Peppers
Asparagus with Cheese
Orange-Honey Cookies

Cheese Straws
Venetian Rice Soup
Chicken with Artichoke Hearts
Sliced Peaches with Apricot Sauce

Summer means the south of France. The simple pleasures of pinewoods and sea are still to be found; olive trees, ink-dark cypresses, gardens, and groves full of lemon, orange, and tangerine trees are all there.

Bell Peppers Vinaigrette
Veal Chops with Basil
Potato Pancakes
Macédoine of Summer Fruits

Tomatoes with Gorgonzola
Lamb Kebabs
Corn Fritters
Fresh Fruit with Zabaione

Neapolitan Omelet
Shrimp Salad with Tomatoes and
    Capers
Ice Cream with Raspberry Sauce

Mushrooms with White Wine
Mixed Green Salad
Summer Spaghetti
Rich Chocolate Cookies

Prawn and Melon Salad
Grilled Chicken with Summer
    Vegetables
Roman Cornbread
Poached Fresh Figs

Crab Cakes with Caper Sauce
Summer Squash Sauté
Endive Salad
Ginger Cake

FALL MENUS

Fall means the wines of Umbria and the hills near Rome, driving to see the leaves turn, and stopping by the vineyards at harvesttime. The rich amber wine is delightful with homemade bread and thin slices of prosciutto.

Pumpkin Fritters
Chicken with Brandy
Spinach with Prosciutto
Apple Fool

Cheese-Roasted Peppers
Sautéed Squab
Braised Belgian Endive
Oat Cookies

Carrot Soup
Veal Kidneys Sauté
Watercress and Potato Salad
Glazed Bananas

Fried Cheese
Radicchio Salad
Medallions of Lamb in
    Sweet-and-Sour Sauce
Apples with Cranberries

Seafood Stew with Aïoli Sauce
Artichokes Provençale
Hazelnut Thins

Risotto with Fresh Herbs
Mixed Green Salad
Fillet of Beef with Vermouth
Carrot-Orange Cake

Winter means Switzerland with clean, white snow, cold, thin alpine air, and hearty fare. There are spicy sausages, mustards, cheeses, and creamy chocolate. Hot fondues are served with robust, full-bodied red wines and crusty bread.

Salmon Terrine
Potato Soup with Swiss Cheese
Fennel Niçoise
Rich Chocolate Dessert

Curried Bananas
Turkey Fillets with Marsala
Romaine and Roquefort Salad
Almond Cookies

Green Zucchini Soup
Veal Scallops with Apples and
   Calvados
Onion-Potato Purée
Sesame Seed Wafers

Savory Shrimp
Roast Quail
Orange-Ginger Sauce
Glazed Winter Vegetables
Raisin Wafers

Thick Vegetable Soup
Capellini with Fish Sauce
Endive and Orange Salad
White Chocolate Squares

Chicken and Duck Liver Pâté
Pork Chops with Red Wine
Leeks by the Bunch
Winter Fruit Dessert

Index